The 7-Day Quilt

To start with, it is helpful to learn the basic anatomy of the quilt you are making. This quilt consists of three layers—the top layer, the batting layer, and the backing layer. The quilt top is a sheet of patches sewn together, the batting layer is a bonded sheet of synthetic polyester fiber cut the same size as your finished quilt top, and the backing layer is a solid piece of fabric slightly larger than your finished quilt top.

When you have sewn your quilt top together, this top is placed on top of the batting and backing. These three separate layers form a "sandwich," which can be held together by running stitches (called *quilting*) or by a stitch made at each junction point (called *tufting*). Because quilting takes more time to learn and to do, the quilt you are making by the *7-Day Quilt Method* will be tufted.

Having pinpointed these facts in your mind, you are ready to move on to the *Glossary*.

The top layer consists of a sheet of patches sewn together. This forms your quilt top.

The batting layer is a bonded sheet of synthetic polyester fiber cut the same size as your finished quilt top.

The backing layer is a solid piece of fabric cut slightly larger than the size of your finished quilt top.

Glossary

A

Appliqué: To apply a small piece of fabric onto a larger piece of fabric. Also, appliqué is used to patch a worn spot on a quilt, by placing a patch of fabric larger than the worn spot on top, turning all the outer edges under ¼ inch (0.64 cm.), and sewing into place.

B

Backing: The bottom layer of a quilt. It is usually cut from a solid or printed fabric and measures slightly larger than the dimensions of the quilt top.

Baste: To sew together temporarily.

Batiste: A sheer, soft-finished cotton fabric woven in a plain weave. This fabric is too finely woven to be used in your quilt.

Batting: A sheet of bonded 100% polyester fiber filler. The batting is sandwiched between the quilt top and backing and gives the quilt body and warmth. A "batt" was originally a thin layer of cotton used by pioneer women in their quilts.

Blend: An interchangeable term, in this case meaning combined with cotton. Examples are Dacron® and cotton, polyester and cotton, etc.

Block: An entire design made from several different shapes, usually measuring 8 to 14 inches (20.48 to 35.84 cm.) square. Examples can be seen in *What's Next?* (*see page 109*).

Broadcloth: A plain, closely woven fabric with a slightly ribbed effect. It can be a print or a plain solid color. In medium weight, it is a good choice as a fabric for your quilt top.

Brown-paper pattern: A full-scale paper pattern on which you lay out your fabric patches to form a design pattern.

C

Calico: A plainly woven fabric of low- to medium-weight cotton printed in small-scale patterns. The medium-weight fabric is an excellent choice to use in combination with other fabrics throughout your quilt top. Because calico patterns are so small in scale, they can be used as part of your quilt top and also as a backing fabric.

Challis: A printed or dyed fabric woven in a plain or twill weave, giving a soft finish and a slight nap. Challis is a good choice for your quilt top. If coordinated carefully with other challis prints, it can make an exciting and unusual quilt top.

Chintz: A fabric woven with a high thread count, resembling fine sheeting. Printed in bold floral or geometric designs, it is often given a permanent or semipermanent glaze (known as *glazed chintz*). This medium-weight fabric can be used in your quilt top if carefully interspersed with other fabrics. A floral design patch can make a beautiful center motif.

Clip: To cut through the edge of fabric for a certain distance before ripping.

Color story: A plan that you have developed, based on your favorite colors and your room colors on walls, furniture, floor coverings, and accessories.

Corduroy: A ribbed pile fabric with a high, soft luster. This fabric is generally unsuitable for a quilt top, as it is too heavy and ravels too easily.

Crosswise grain: This is at right angles to the lengthwise grain of your fabric and runs from selvage to selvage.

D

Denim: A durable fabric of the twill family, too heavy to use in your quilt top.

Design pattern: The design for your quilt top that you have created on your brown-paper pattern, paste-up pattern, or graph-paper pattern.

Dimity: A sheer dyed or printed fabric of plain weave. This fabric is too lightweight to be used in your quilt top.

Duck: This term covers a wide range of fabric types, such as army duck, etc. It is much too heavy in weight for your quilt top.

E

Easing in: This is a way of fitting fabric patches together when one is slightly larger than another. It is done by fitting the larger patch to the smaller by gently pressing in the excess fabric with your thumb.

G

Gingham: A light- to medium-weight fabric, of which there are endless variations in color and design. Most popular of all is checked gingham. Medium-weight gingham is an excellent choice for your quilt top.

Graph-paper pattern: A sheet of graph paper with ¼-inch (0.64-cm.) grids on which you can work out your quilt-top design.

J

Junction points: The places where the corners of your patches meet exactly.

L

Lengthwise grain: The grain that runs parallel to the selvage of a piece of fabric.

M

Madras: A fabric usually woven in plaids, stripes, or pattern design. It can be used in your quilt top, if coordinated carefully with other colors and patterns you have selected.

Miter: A fold made at a 45-degree angle at each corner of the quilt.

Muslin: A coarse type of cotton fabric resembling lightweight sheeting, sometimes called "unbleached muslin." It can be used in your quilt top if you purchase the preshrunk type or a 50%-Dacron®-50% cotton blend. It makes a good, inexpensive backing fabric, too.

N

Nap: A surface fuzziness on fabrics such as velvets and corduroys that is the result of a brushing process applied to the fabric after it has been woven. Patches cut from napped fabric will vary from one patch to another, if they are not all cut in the same direction.

O

Off grain: Patches whose lengthwise and crosswise grains are not at right angles.

One-way design: A design printed on a piece of fabric, running in only one direction.

On grain: A term referring to patches that have been perfectly cut when ripped from strips whose lengthwise and crosswise grains are at right angles.

Organdy: A thin, transparent, lightweight fabric that is too sheer to use in a quilt top.

Outing flannel: A light- or medium-weight fabric with slight nap on both sides. It is woven in plaids, checks, stripes, or printed with patterns. It can be used in your quilt top if coordinated very carefully with other fabrics. Using all flannels will create a soft look. It is especially handsome when used in a baby's or child's quilt.

Oxford cloth: A plainly woven fabric of medium and heavy weights. Dyed in solid colors, it is often used in shirting fabrics. This fabric can be used in your quilt top, especially if you want to also use men's old shirts that are still strongly woven. Care must be taken, however, to coordinate this fabric carefully with other fabrics you plan to use in your quilt top.

P

Paste-up Pattern: A small-scale paper pattern cut 20 by 20 inches (51.20 by 51.20 cm.) and ruled in with 1- by 1-inch (2.56- by 2.56-cm.) squares.

Patch: A piece of fabric, which is cut out using a template, that when joined with other patches forms your quilt top. This patch could be a perfect square or of rectangular shape.

Percale: A plainly woven, medium-weight fabric. It can be dyed or printed and is an excellent fabric to use in your quilt top.

Piecing: Sometimes quilts are composed of square, diamond, triangular, or rectangular shapes. Piecing is the method used for joining these shapes together by pinning, sewing, and pressing.

Poplin: A plain, closely woven fabric, woven of heavier threads than broadcloth. It is mainly dyed in solid colors, but is sometimes printed. Because of its heavier weight, it is better not to use it in the body of your quilt top. However, it makes an excellent solid-colored backing fabric.

Q

Quilting: A way of anchoring the three layers of a quilt together with tiny running stitches.

R

Running stitch: When applied to quilting the stitch is made by inserting the needle through all three quilt layers. As the needle is passed in and out and the thread is pulled through, stitches are formed.

S

Seam allowance: The distance from the cut edge of the fabric to where your stitching line begins. You will use a ½-inch (1.28-cm.) seam allowance when sewing your quilt top.

Seersucker: A plainly woven fabric in either a medium or heavy weight, with a woven crinkled effect, in plaids, checks, or stripes. It can be used in your quilt top, but looks best if a whole quilt is made from it, with carefully coordinated colors and patterns. If you do mix seersucker with plain flat cottons and cotton blends, great care must be taken in thinking out your total design pattern.

Selvage: The finished woven edge found on each vertical side of a piece of fabric.

Sheetings: Plainly woven fabrics often used to make bed sheets. Medium weight is excellent to use both in your quilt top and as a backing fabric.

Square off: To straighten the outer edge of your quilt top, creating the illusion of a perfect square or rectangle.

Stitch: To sew either by machine or by hand.

Synthetic: A term commonly used for any fabric made of man-made fibers.

T

Template: A full-scale pattern made of cardboard used to outline patches for cutting.

Terry cloth: A fabric woven on a loom, which produces uncut loops on both sides. Because this fabric is heavy and ravels easily, it is unsuitable for your quilt top.

Tufting: A stitch that is used to secure the three layers of a quilt together. The stitch can be made at each corner junction point or in the center of each patch.

V

Velveteen: A plain or twill woven fabric which has a glowing, lustrous pile. This fabric may be dyed a solid color or printed. It is not suitable fabric to use in your quilt top, because it ravels, stretches easily, and has a nap that may cause problems. If you do decide to make your whole quilt top of velveteen, you should be a seasoned sewer and a careful worker.

W

Weft thread: The horizontal threads, often called *filler threads*, that run from selvage to selvage.

Your Toolbox

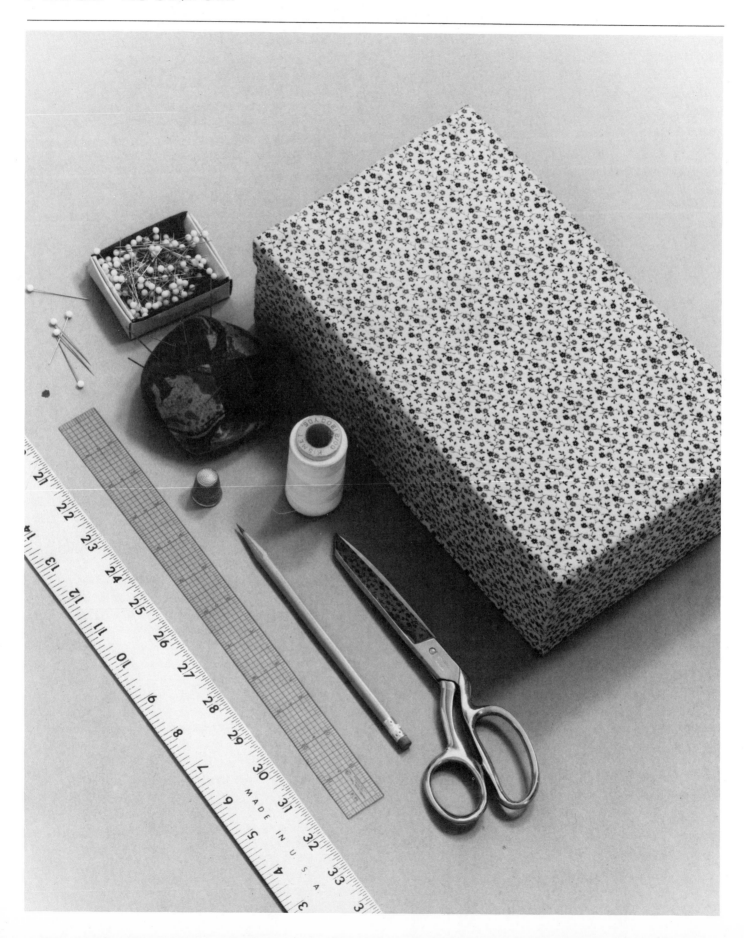

In every craft it is necessary to assemble certain tools before you begin.

I find it helpful to keep all of my tools in one place. Some of my students keep their tools in a shoebox, a sewing basket, or an envelope. I find the shoe box most convenient, and, if you cover the outer surface with a colorful fabric such as calico (which I glue on), you won't be embarrassed to leave your toolbox out. There is nothing more frustrating than to set the time aside to work and then to waste time gathering the tools. If you keep your tools together and put them in a special place, you will never have that problem.

Mentioned in this section are some of the tools that help make your work easier. An excellent place to begin is with a good pair of scissors.

Some of my students come to class with diamonds on their fingers and a broken-down pair of scissors in their hands. By "broken-down" I mean that the blades can hardly open and close, much less cut a straight line. Treat yourself to a super-fine pair of scissors, 8 to 10 inches (20.48 to 25.60 cm.) long. The blades should be long, smooth, and even, and should open and close easily. (If the blades do not, either take the scissors back or try having someone with strong muscles turn the screw counterclockwise until the blades open and shut easily.)

If you have a good pair of scissors that seem dull, take them to a reliable person to be sharpened. When you pick them up, make certain that they cut well by testing them on a scrap of fabric before paying for them.

Believe it or not, some people try to use garden shears, paper scissors, or even kitchen shears (used for cutting chicken, fish, etc.) to cut fabric. Your scissors should be lightweight, well-balanced, but strong, and of a kind that can be easily sharpened. (Some foreign-made scissors are well designed, but can't be sharpened, and are made of a thin quality of steel which bends easily.) So treat yourself to a super-fine pair of scissors. Later, you'll thank me for being such a nag.

TOOLS TO BUY

1. Scissors
   8 to 10 inches long, sharpened to cut a clean line
2. Pins
   1¼ inch (3.20 cm.)

3. Needles:
   Eight to ten sharp needles for hand-sewing
   Milliners' 3/9 needles for basting
   Embroidery crewel needles, size 7, for tufting and embroidering
4. Thread
   Purchase cotton-covered polyester (comes in only one size), which can be used on light- and medium-weight fabrics.
5. Thimble
   Use one that fits easily on your finger, but that doesn't shift. If you have never sewn with a thimble before, give it a try. You may be pleasantly surprised to discover how much more quickly and easily you are able to hand-sew.
6. Transparent plastic ruler
   You need a 12- by 1-or-2-inch (30.72- by 2.56-or-5.12-cm.) type called a *C-Thru ruler.* Art-supply stores or large stationery stores often have these.
7. Wood or metal yardstick
   Try the local hardware store first, then the tool department at local department stores.
8. Sharpened #2 pencils

SUPPLIES FOR MAKING YOUR TEMPLATE

1. Rubber cement or glue
2. Heavy piece of cardboard
3. Sheet of graph paper
4. Two telephone books to use as weights

OTHER SUPPLIES FOR FINISHING OFF YOUR QUILT

1. Backing fabric
   This should be 8 inches longer and wider than your finished quilt top.
2. Batting
   This should be the size of your finished quilt. Many major department stores or large dime stores carry quilt batting. Some stores have a selection of different sizes, so be sure to know your quilt size before you buy.
3. A ball of Knit-Cro-Sheen
   This is used for tufting your quilt. It should pick up and coordinate with the colors in your quilt top and should be bought only after you finish your quilt top. If you are not sure of the color to buy, pin swatches of all the fabrics that you have used in your quilt top on a plain sheet of white paper, as seen on page 29. That way, you can match your Knit-Cro-Sheen exactly to the fabrics in your quilt top.

Making and Using Your Template

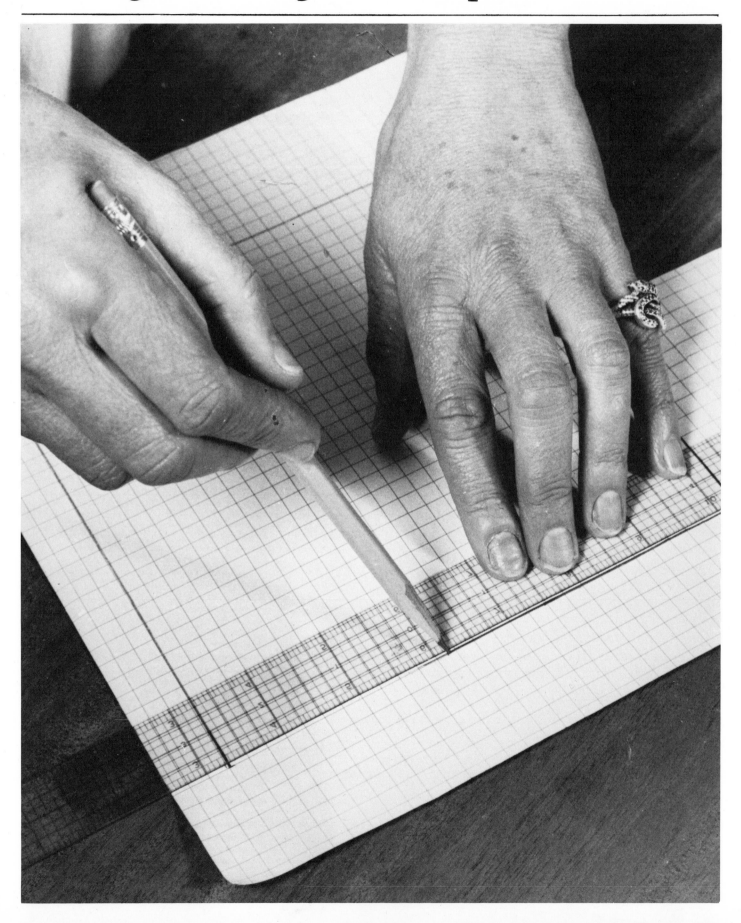

Each semester, at the beginning of my quilting classes, one of the questions most often asked by my students is, "What is a template, and how can I make one?"

A template is a full-scale pattern made from a stiff piece of cardboard, which you use to outline your patches on a piece of fabric for cutting.

Let me stress here that when cutting out your template it is imperative to cut exactly on the cutting lines, as indicated. If your template is even 1/16 inch (0.16 cm.) off, it is crooked. That means that the patches marked in with the template will be crooked and that your quilt top will be crooked, too. The instructions that follow will tell you how to make a template:

1. On graph paper, mark out in pencil a 7- by 7-inch (17.92- by 17.92-cm.) square with your C-Thru ruler, as shown.

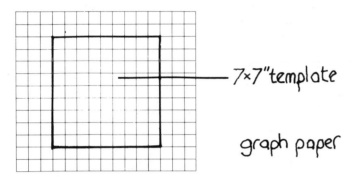

The 7-by-7-inch square measured out on graph paper.

2. Cut out this 7- by 7-inch (17.92- by 17.92-cm.) square on the marked pencil lines, making certain that you cut exactly on the lines you have just marked in. (Remember: If you are off, your patches will be crooked.)

3. Take this 7- by 7-inch (17.92- by 17.92-cm.) square and glue it onto a stiff piece of cardboard, as shown.

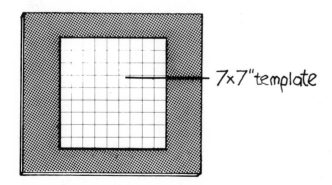

The 7-by-7-inch square glued onto cardboard.

4. Cut around this 7- by 7-inch (17.92- by 17.92-cm.) square with paper scissors. This 7- by 7-inch square is your template.

5. Mark in a ½-inch (1.28-cm.) seam allowance on your template, using your C-Thru ruler. This ½-inch seam allowance represents the line on which you will later sew. Later, after you have marked your patches for cutting, you will cut along this seam allowance line to remove the inner section. This will give you a windowpane template with which you will be able to mark off a ½-inch seam allowance on your patches.

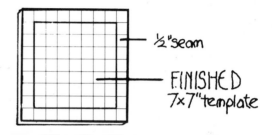

The finished 7-by-7-inch template mounted on cardboard with seam allowance marked in.

If you would like a quicker and simpler way to make your template, I have provided one for you, which you need only cut out and paste on a piece of stiff cardboard. You'll find it on page 113.

Quilt Fact Sheets

As you do the measuring for your quilt, fill in the blank spaces below. Then you can easily refer back to these dimensions as needed.

QUILT 1

1. Mattress dimensions
   Width _____
   Length _____
   Depth _____
   Overhang _____
   Additional measurements _____
2. Finished quilt size _____
3. Number of rows in quilt top
   Horizontal _____
   Vertical _____
4. Total number of patches to cut _____
5. How much fabric to buy for quilt top _____

6. Number of patches to cut of each color and pattern
   _____
   _____
7. How much batting to buy for quilt (same size as finished quilt) (see #2, above) _____
8. How much backing to buy for quilt _____

QUILT 2

1. Mattress dimensions
   Width _____
   Length _____
   Depth _____
   Overhang _____
   Additional measurements _____
2. Finished quilt size _____
3. Number of rows in quilt top
   Horizontal _____
   Vertical _____
4. Total number of patches to cut _____
5. How much fabric to buy for quilt top _____

6. Number of patches to cut of each color and pattern
   _____
   _____
7. How much batting to buy for quilt (same size as finished quilt (see #2, above) _____
8. How much backing to buy for quilt _____

QUILT 3

1. Mattress dimensions
   Width _____
   Length _____
   Depth _____
   Overhang _____
   Additional measurements _____
2. Finished quilt size _____
3. Number of rows in quilt top
   Horizontal _____
   Vertical _____
4. Total number of patches to cut _____
5. How much fabric to buy for quilt top _____

6. Number of patches to cut of each color and pattern
   _____
   _____
7. How much batting to buy for quilt (same size as finished quilt) (see #2, above) _____
8. How much backing to buy for quilt _____

QUILT 4

1. Mattress dimensions
   Width _____
   Length _____
   Depth _____
   Overhang _____
   Additional measurements _____
2. Finished quilt size _____
3. Number of rows in quilt top
   Horizontal _____
   Vertical _____
4. Total number of patches to cut _____
5. How much fabric to buy for quilt top _____

6. Number of patches to cut of each color and pattern
   _____
   _____
7. How much batting to buy for quilt (same size as finished quilt) (see #2, above) _____
8. How much backing to buy for quilt _____

QUILT 5

1. Mattress dimensions
   Width _____
   Length _____
   Depth _____
   Overhang _____
   Additional measurements _____
2. Finished quilt size _____
3. Number of rows in quilt top
   Horizontal _____
   Vertical _____
4. Total number of patches to cut _____
5. How much fabric to buy for quilt top _____
   _____
6. Number of patches to cut of each color and pattern
   _____
   _____
7. How much batting to buy for quilt (same size as finished quilt) (see #2, above) _____
8. How much backing to buy for quilt _____

QUILT 6

1. Mattress dimensions
   Width _____
   Length _____
   Depth _____
   Overhang _____
   Additional measurements _____
2. Finished quilt size _____
3. Number of rows in quilt top
   Horizontal _____
   Vertical _____
4. Total number of patches to cut _____
5. How much fabric to buy for quilt top _____
   _____
6. Number of patches to cut of each color and pattern
   _____
   _____
7. How much batting to buy for quilt (same size as finished quilt) (see #2, above) _____
8. How much backing to buy for quilt _____

QUILT 7

1. Mattress dimensions
   Width _____
   Length _____
   Depth _____
   Overhang _____
   Additional measurements _____
2. Finished quilt size _____
3. Number of rows in quilt top
   Horizontal _____
   Vertical _____
4. Total number of patches to cut _____
5. How much fabric to buy for quilt top _____
   _____
6. Number of patches to cut of each color and pattern
   _____
   _____
7. How much batting to buy for quilt (same size as finished quilt) (see #2, above) _____
8. How much backing to buy for quilt _____

QUILT 8

1. Mattress dimensions
   Width _____
   Length _____
   Depth _____
   Overhang _____
   Additional measurements _____
2. Finished quilt size _____
3. Number of rows in quilt top
   Horizontal _____
   Vertical _____
4. Total number of patches to cut _____
5. How much fabric to buy for quilt top _____
   _____
6. Number of patches to cut of each color and pattern
   _____
   _____
7. How much batting to buy for quilt (same size as finished quilt) (see #2, above) _____
8. How much backing to buy for quilt _____

Measuring for Your Quilt Size

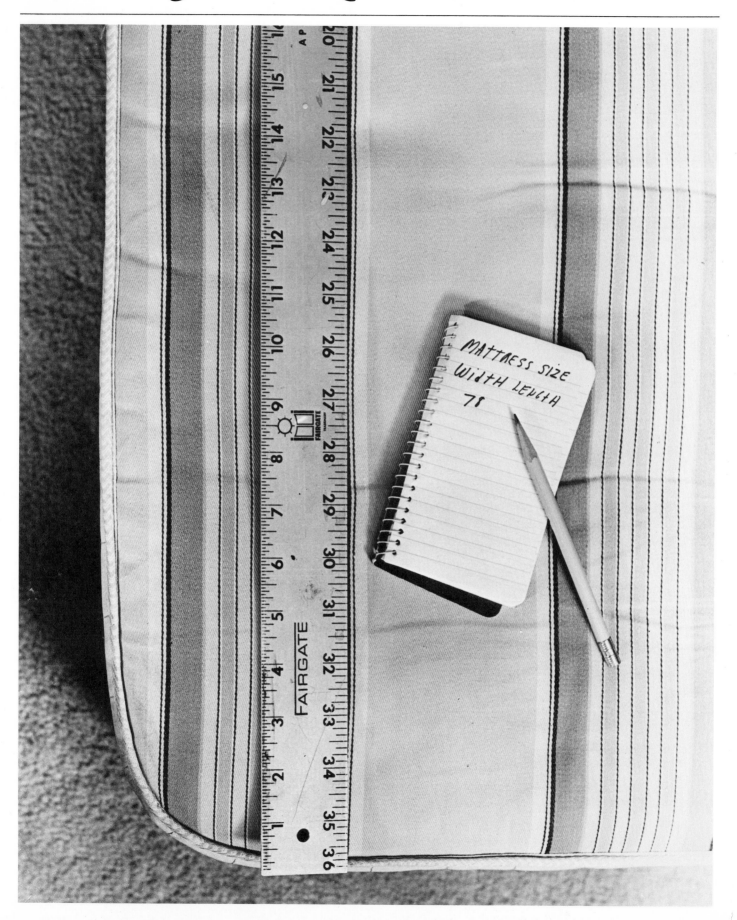

Before proceeding any further, now is the time to do the measuring for your quilt size. The first step is to measure your mattress. (If you are making the quilt for another person as a surprise, see *page 24.*)

Before you begin to measure your mattress, take a look at your Quilt Fact Sheet. As you measure your mattress, write each individual dimension down on this sheet.

1. Width of mattress
   Measure width of mattress from inner corner to inner corner, as shown.

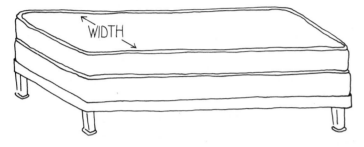

Measure the width of the mattress.

2. Length of mattress
   Measure length of mattress from inner corner to inner corner, as shown.

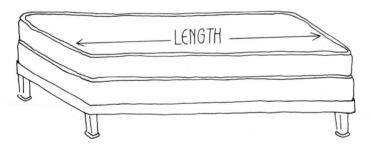

Measure the length of the mattress.

3. Depth of mattress
   Measure the depth (thickness) of mattress, as shown, doubling this dimension to account for both sides of your mattress.

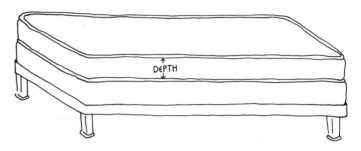

Measure the depth of the mattress.

4. Overhang for quilt
   Measure overhang, which is how far you want your quilt to hang below the edge of mattress. Double this dimension to account for both sides of your mattress.

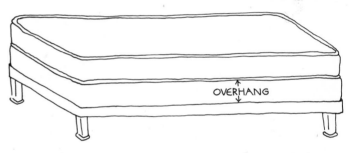

Measure the overhang (the distance quilt is to hang below the mattress).

Now take the dimensions you have written down on your Quilt Fact Sheet and add them up, using the following chart to produce the final measurements for your quilt:

	Width	Length
1. Mattress dimensions	____	____
2. Depth of mattress*	+ ____	+ ____
3. Overhang*	____	____
4. Subtotal	____ ×	____ = ____
5. Additional measurements	____	____
6. Total	____ ×	____ = ____ Your total measurement

*These dimensions—depth of mattress and overhang should be entered in both the width and length columns, as they account for two sides of the mattress at once.

Now ask yourself these practical questions:

1. Do you want the quilt to lie flush against the head-board? If so, eliminate the depth measurement for the head of the mattress (this would be half of the depth measurement in either column).

2. Do you want the quilt to hang to the floor? Then measure from the end of the mattress to the floor, double this dimension, and enter the doubled dimension in both columns for #5, *Additional Measurements.*

3. Do you want the quilt to tuck under the mattress? If so, allow 3 to 4 inches (7.68 to 10.24 cm.), double this dimension, and add to both columns of #5, *Additional Measurements.*

4. Do you want more at the top of the quilt to allow for pillow underlay? Then allow 7 inches (17.92 cm.) and add it to the length measurement *only.*

5. Do you want the quilt to hang 2 inches (5.12 cm.) below a dust ruffle? Then allow 2 inches (5.12 cm.), double it, and enter it in both columns of #5, *Additional Measurements.*

If you are making a quilt for another person far away and can't measure the mattress, or, if you are making a quilt as a surprise gift, a general rule to follow is: Always think larger, rather than smaller. Use the Standard Bed Measurements that follow as a guide and proceed with the calculations just given:

Bed	Size
Double	54 by 74 inches (1.38 by 1.89 m.)
Queen	60 by 74–84 inches (1.54 by 1.89-2.15 m.)
King	64 by 74 inches (1.64 by 1.89 m.) or 74 by 84 inches (1.89 by 2.15 m.)
Single	39 by 74 inches (99.84 cm. by 1.89 m.)
Children's	48 by 68 inches (1.23 by 1.74 m.)
Bunk or cot	33 by 74 inches (84.48 cm. by 1.89 m.)
Infant's	20 by 36 inches (51.20 by 92.16 cm.) or 36 by 54 inches (92.16 cm. by 1.38 m.)

Remember that the *total* width and length measurements you've computed represent your finished quilt dimensions (unless you wish to have a wider border, which you will learn about later on). Now take your Quilt Fact Sheet and write your finished quilt dimensions in the space marked *Finished Quilt Size*.

Your next step is to compute the number of rows needed for your quilt top. Divide each dimension (width and length) by six, as shown:

$$6\overline{)\text{Width}} = \text{Number of vertical rows in quilt top}$$

$$6\overline{)\text{Length}} = \text{Number of horizontal rows in quilt top}$$

The reason you divide by six is that, although your patches will be cut 7 by 7 inches (17.92 by 17.92 cm.), there is a ½-inch (1.28-cm.) seam allowance all around, which means that your finished patch actually measures 6 by 6 inches (15.36 by 15.36 cm.). Of course, if you have decided to make your patches larger or smaller than 6 inches, you would divide by whatever number you had chosen. In any case, always round off the number of rows to an *odd* number, because you need an odd number of rows in your quilt top to create a center focal point.

After dividing each dimension by six, you will have the number of vertical and horizontal rows in your quilt top. Write down the number of vertical and horizontal rows in the space provided in the Quilt Fact Sheet.

To figure out the total number of patches needed for your quilt top multiply the number of vertical rows in your quilt by the number of horizontal rows:

Vertical rows

×

Horizontal rows

—————————————————

Number of patches in quilt top

This total represents the total number of patches in your quilt top. Write this number down on your Quilt Fact Sheet under #4, *Total Number of Patches To Cut*.

Choosing Your Colors

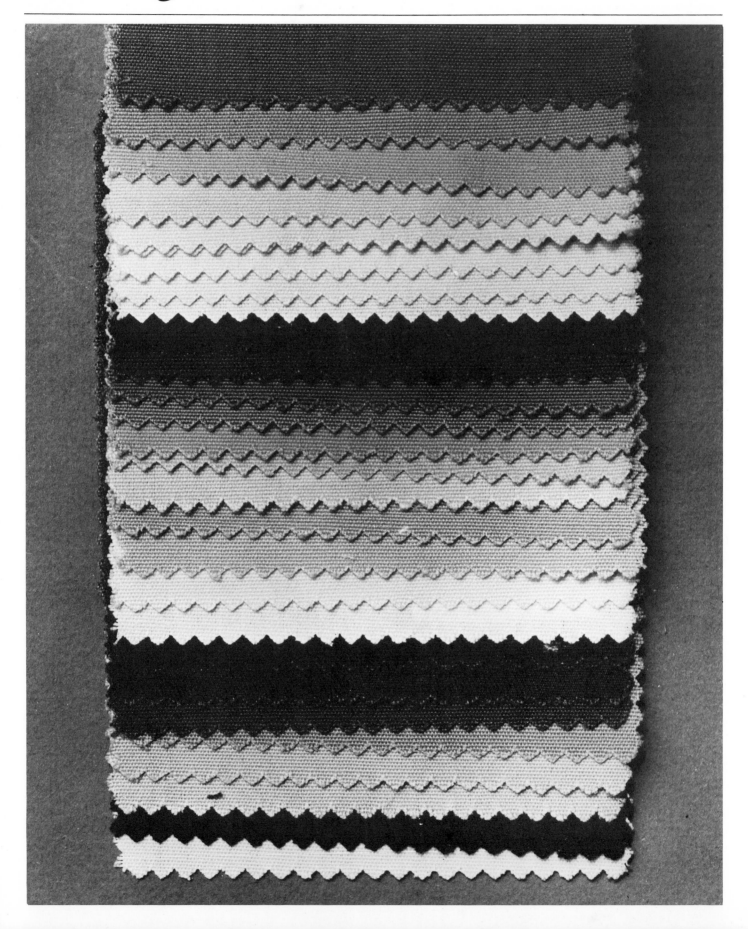

After you have gathered all your fabrics together, determine which need to be washed, and why. If you have any 100% cotton fabrics, they should be washed in the hot-water cycle of your washing machine. Should you be uncertain of a fabric's content, throw it in the washing machine as an extra precaution against shrinkage. After you have washed and dried your fabrics, take them out of the dryer immediately and hang them up in order to avoid wrinkles. If fabrics seem wrinkled, press them lightly with a steam iron. Your fabrics will then be ready for marking and cutting into patches.

How do you know how many patches of each color and pattern to cut? Divide the total number of patches in your quilt top by the number of colors or patterns of fabric you have. For example, if you have 175 patches in your quilt top and eight different colors or patterns, divide 175 by eight. If you discover as you lay out patches on your paper pattern (see *page 61*) that you would like more of a particular color or pattern, then simply cut more of just that color or pattern.

Lay out all your fabrics, side by side, and make sure they are all compatible.

A Gallery of Quilts

2

2
The Signal Quilt
Designed and made by Josephine Rogers
1978   New York City
74 by 84 inches (1.89 by 2.15 m.)
   Bold stop-and-go colors of red and green, shot with yellow,
   create drama in this geometric pattern.
Cotton blends

1
The Cowboy Quilt
Designed by Josephine Rogers, made by Barbara Nolan
1978   New York City
52 by 63 inches (1.33 by 1.61 m.)
   Bandanna- and calico-printed fabrics are combined with a
   large realistic cowboy pattern. Notice that this realistic motif
   is a one-way design, therefore requiring a bit more work and
   fabric. The cowboys galloping throughout the quilt, however,
   provide an exciting sense of movement.
Cotton blends

19

20

21
The Five-Cross Quilt
Designed and made by Christa Simpson
1978   New York City
74 by 84 inches (1.89 by 2.15 m.)
This quilt has been made entirely from red and white floral, striped, and dotted patterns. Notice the symmetry of the design pattern and how Christa has used the striped cross as her central motif, which repeats in each of the four corners. Christa told me that she loves borders. She must—because she has used four different borders on this strikingly original quilt.
Cotton blends

22

23

24

25

22
The Bandanna Print Quilt
Designed by Josephine Rogers, made by Marian Bartholomew
1978   New York City
70 by 75 inches (1.79 by 1.92 m.)
In this quilt yellow and blue calicos intermingle with a red bandanna print, forming contrasting diamond-shaped patterns. A simple border (which cannot be seen in this photograph) is made from yellow and blue calico patches.
Cotton blends

23
American One-Patch Tablecloth
Designed by Josephine Rogers, made by Jan Jenicek
1978   New York City
At last, tablecloths are back! Everyone is dressing up their tables these days. Seen here are cool pastels intermingled with startling primary colors of midnight blue, sunshine yellow, and fiery red. A midnight blue border frames this tablecloth.
Cotton blends

26
Garden of Eden Kitchen Curtains
Designed by Josephine Rogers, made by Marian Bartholomew
1978   New York City
These curtains could have been found in the Garden of Eden. Notice that Adam has taken a bite of the forbidden fruit, which offers the humor for the center motif. Checks, stripes, and floral patterns are juxtaposed in this design pattern, which is finished off by a dazzling navy blue and turquoise border.
100% cotton and cotton blends

24
The American Indian Quilt
Designed and made by Josephine Rogers
1978   New York City
60 by 84 inches (1.54 by 2.15 m.)
Who says that turquoise blue, royal purple, and berry red can't be teamed together? Notice how the patches of royal purple seem to march across the raised field of turquoise blue, which has been tufted in the center of each patch. Alternating bands of berry red and turquoise blue delineate the spatial area on the quilt itself and reappear to create an elegant border.
Cotton blends

25
Sunshine and Shadow
Designed and made by Josephine Rogers
1977   New York City
60 by 84 inches (1.54 by 2.15 m.)
The unlikely combination of black, pink, and skipper blue is boldly used in this Amish-inspired pattern.
Cotton blends

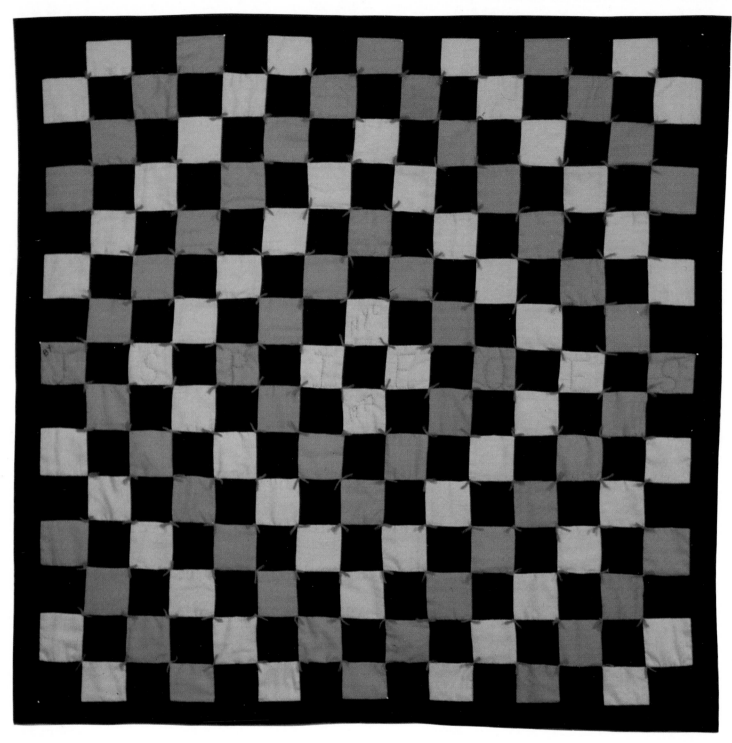

27
Sunshine and Shadow, Baby Style
Designed and made by Josephine Rogers
1977   **New York City**
33 by 34 inches (84.48 by 87.04 cm.)
   Who said that baby quilts have to be made in pastel colors?
   Not the Amish! Stark black contrasts with shades of pink to
   create drama in this baby-quilt version of the pattern. Dark
   red yarn was used for the tufting.
Cotton blends

Creating Your Design Pattern

One of the most important steps in quilt-making is the creation of the quilt-top design. One of the five easy design patterns given in the next few pages might be just what you need, or you might want to try your hand at planning your own design. In any case, there are four basic ways to find your design:

Choose from the brown-paper-pattern method, the paste-up-pattern method, and the graph-paper-pattern method.

1. Choose one of the five easy design patterns given here.
2. Use the brown-paper-pattern method.
3. Use the paste-up-pattern method.
4. Use the graph-paper-pattern method.

Before deciding which method you want to use, you may want to go over the five easy design patterns that follow. The designs are simple and attractive. Four of these patterns call for only three or four different fabrics, while the fifth pattern provides an economical way for you to use scrap fabrics. But remember, each one is for a specific size mattress. If you do want to plan your own design, the method you choose will depend mostly on how much room you have. If you want to try a design pattern where patches are cut and laid out to full scale and you have the room to do it, my brown-paper-pattern method might appeal to you. If you choose my paste-up-pattern method, you will be working on a small scale, which is a convenient way of working for people who have only a small work space. If, on the other hand, you want to make your quilt top of solid-colored fabrics, the simplest way is the graph-paper-pattern method.

The following are some original design patterns I've developed, which I think are both handsome and easy to follow. If you want to develop your own pattern, skip over them completely and read on.

DESIGN PATTERN 1

1. This quilt is for a 54- by 74-inch (1.38- by 1.89-m.) mattress (double-bed size).
2. This design pattern consists of 195 patches in all.
3. For this design pattern cut ninety-eight patches of a light color, forty-nine patches of a medium color, and forty-eight patches of a dark color.
4. Remember, the solid-colored patches used in this design pattern are only an example. They are interchangeable with any printed fabric that you may choose to use.

Colors	Amount of Fabric (36-inch)	Amount of Fabric (45-inch)
Light color	4 yards (3.68 m.)	3 yards (2.76 m.)
Medium color	3 yards (2.76 m.)	2 yards (1.84 m.)
Dark color	3 yards (2.76 m.)	2 yards (1.84 m.)

*Most cotton fabrics run 36 inches (92.16 cm.) wide, while cotton blends run 45 inches (1.15 m.) wide. You can figure on getting twenty-five 7- by 7-inch (17.92- by 17.92-cm.) patches from 1 yard (92.16 cm.) of 36-inch-wide fabric, and thirty 7- by 7-inch patches from 1 yard of 45-inch-wide fabric.

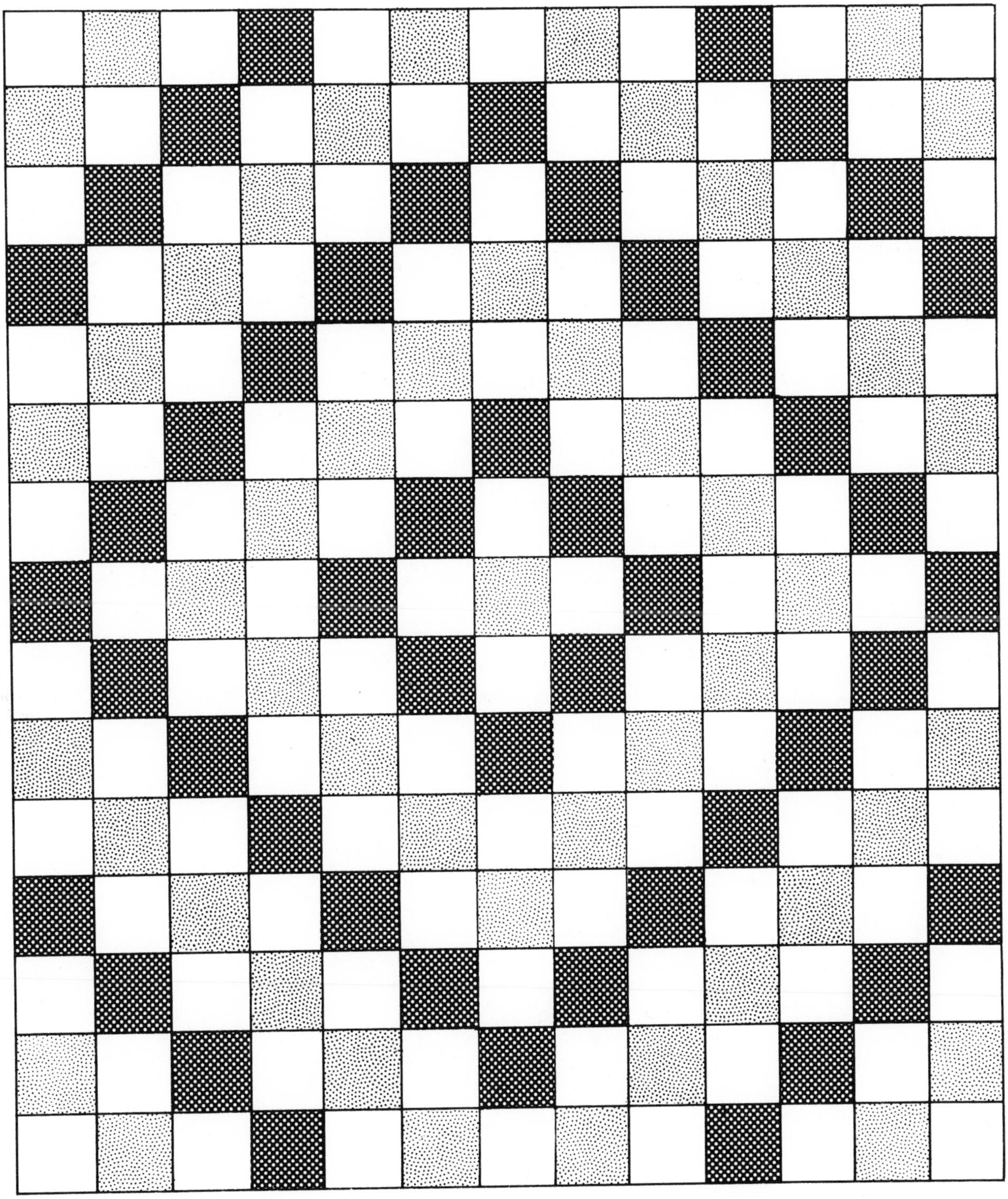

DESIGN PATTERN 2

1. This quilt is for a 54- by 74-inch (1.38- by 1.89-m.) mattress (double-bed size).
2. This design pattern consists of 195 patches in all.
3. For this design pattern cut 124 patches of a light color, twenty-eight patches of a medium color, thirty-three patches of a dark color, and ten patches of a very dark color (this could be black, dark brown, navy blue, dark purple, maroon, or any dark color you choose to use).
4. Remember, the solid-colored patches used in this design pattern are only an example. They are interchangeable with any printed fabric that you may choose to use.

Colors	Amount of Fabric (36-inch)	Amount of Fabric (45-inch)
Light color	5½ yards (5.07 m.)	4½ yards (4.15 m.)
Medium color	1¼ yards (1.15 m.)	1 yard (92.16 cm.)
Dark color	1½ yards (1.38 m.)	1¼ yards (1.15 m.)
Very dark color	½ yard (46.08 cm.)	½ yard (46.08 cm.)

*Most cotton fabrics run 36 inches (92.16 cm.) wide, while cotton blends run 45 inches (1.15 m.) wide. You can figure on getting twenty-five 7- by 7-inch (17.92- by 17.92-cm.) patches from 1 yard (92.16 cm.) of 36-inch-wide fabric, and thirty 7- by 7-inch patches from 1 yard of 45-inch-wide fabric.

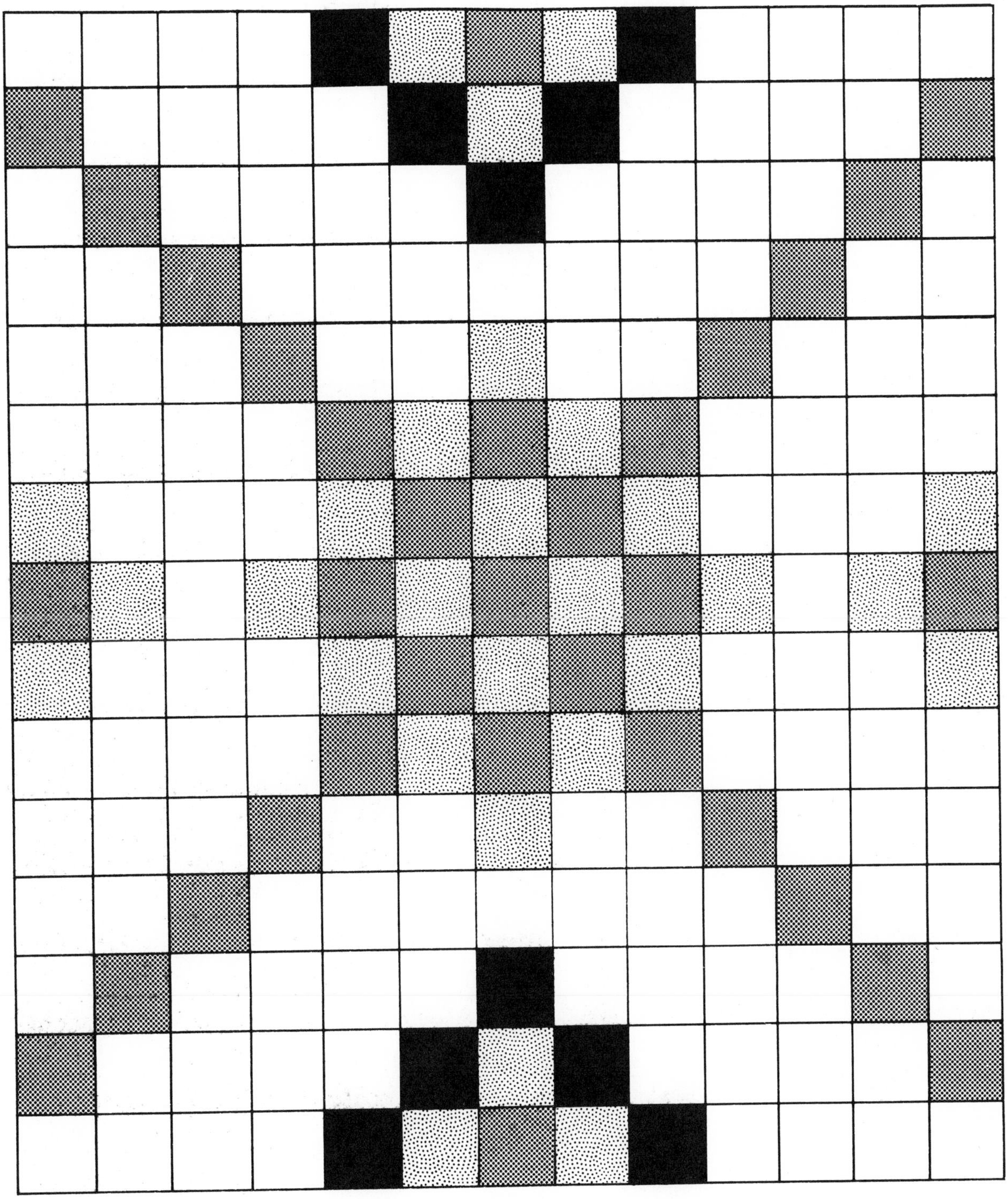

DESIGN PATTERN 3

1. This quilt is for a 54- by 74-inch (1.38- by 1.89-m.) mattress (double-bed size).
2. This design consists of 195 patches in all.
3. For this design pattern cut 118 patches of a light color, twenty-four patches of a medium color, twenty-five patches of a dark color, and twenty-eight patches of a very dark color (this could be black, dark brown, navy blue, dark purple, maroon, or any dark color you choose to use.
4. Remember, the solid-colored patches used in this design pattern are only an example. They are interchangeable with any printed fabric that you may choose to use.

Colors	Amount of Fabric (36-inch)	Amount of Fabric (45-inch)
Light color	5 yards (4.6 m.)	4½ yards (4.15 m.)
Medium color	1 yard (92.16 cm.)	1 yard (92.16 cm.)
Dark color	1⅛ yards (1.1 m.)	1 yard (92.16 cm.)
Very dark color	1¼ yards (1.15 m.)	1 yard (92.16 cm.)

*Most cotton fabrics run 36 inches (92.16 cm.) wide, while cotton blends run 45 inches (1.15 m.) wide. You can figure on getting twenty-five 7- by 7-inch (17.92- by 17.92-cm.) patches from 1 yard (92.16 cm.) of 36-inch-wide fabric, and thirty 7- by 7-inch patches from 1 yard of 45-inch-wide fabric.

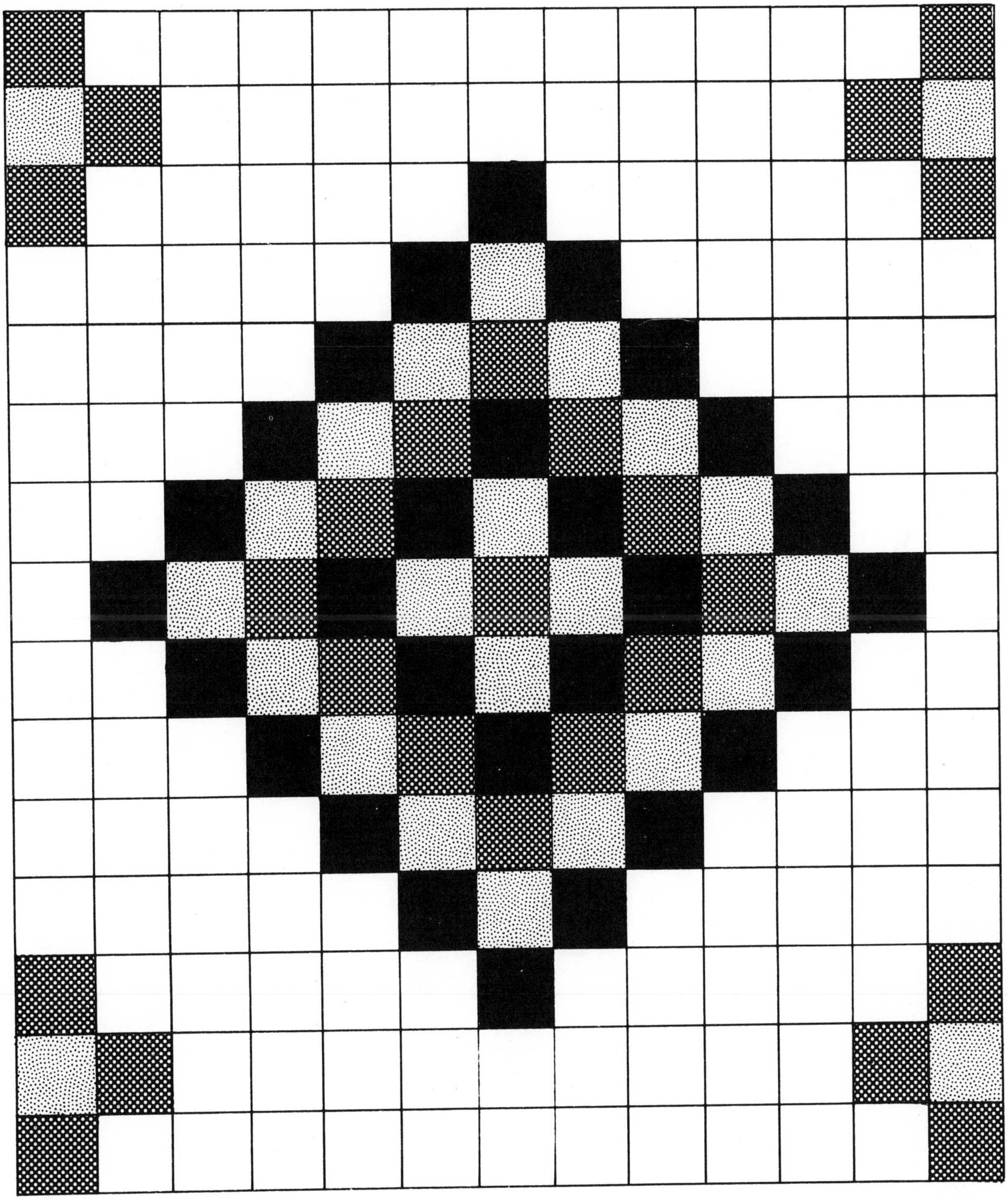

DESIGN PATTERN 4

1. This quilt is for a 54- by 74-inch (1.38- by 1.89-m.) mattress (double-bed size).
2. This design pattern consists of 195 patches in all.
3. For this design pattern cut forty-eight patches of floral print, fifty-nine patches of a medium color and eighty-eight patches of a dark color.

Colors	Amount of Fabric (36-inch)	Amount of Fabric (45-inch)
Floral print	2 yards (1.84 m.)	1¾ yards (1.6 m.)
Medium color	2½ yards (2.3 m.)	2¼ yards (2.07 m.)
Dark color	4 yards (3.68 m.)	3¼ yards (3 m.)

*Most cotton fabrics run 36 inches (92.16 cm.) wide, while cotton blends run 45 inches (1.15 m.) wide. You can estimate getting twenty-five 7- by 7-inch (17.92-17.92-cm.) patches from 1 yard (92.16 cm.) of 36-inch-wide fabric, and thirty 7- by 7-inch patches from 1 yard of 45-inch-wide fabric.

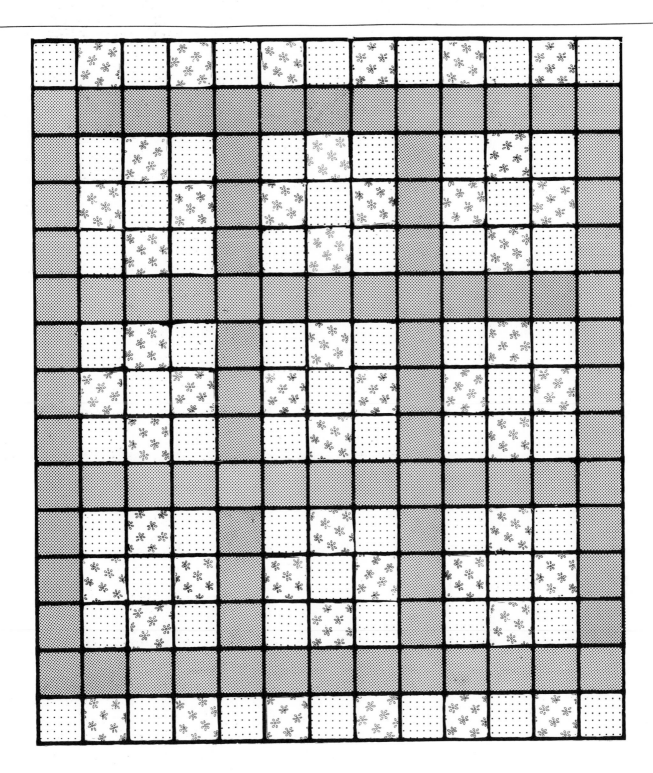

DESIGN PATTERN 5:
THE AMERICAN ONE-PATCH QUILT

Get out your scrap bag, because here's a chance to have some fun by using up some of the scraps of fabric you've been saving. If you just have one small scrap of a fabric you simply love, try using it as your center motif. From there, experiment, using florals, checks, stripes, dots, and even solid-colored fabrics, as long as they all coordinate with your color story. Don't make the mistake here of using fabrics you don't like just to economize. You will be living with your quilt for a long time.

When selecting your fabrics, lay them out side by side, as I have done on *page 31*. That way, you can easily see the scale of patterns whether or not the colors coordinate well together. If you have any doubts about a particular fabric, simply don't use it.

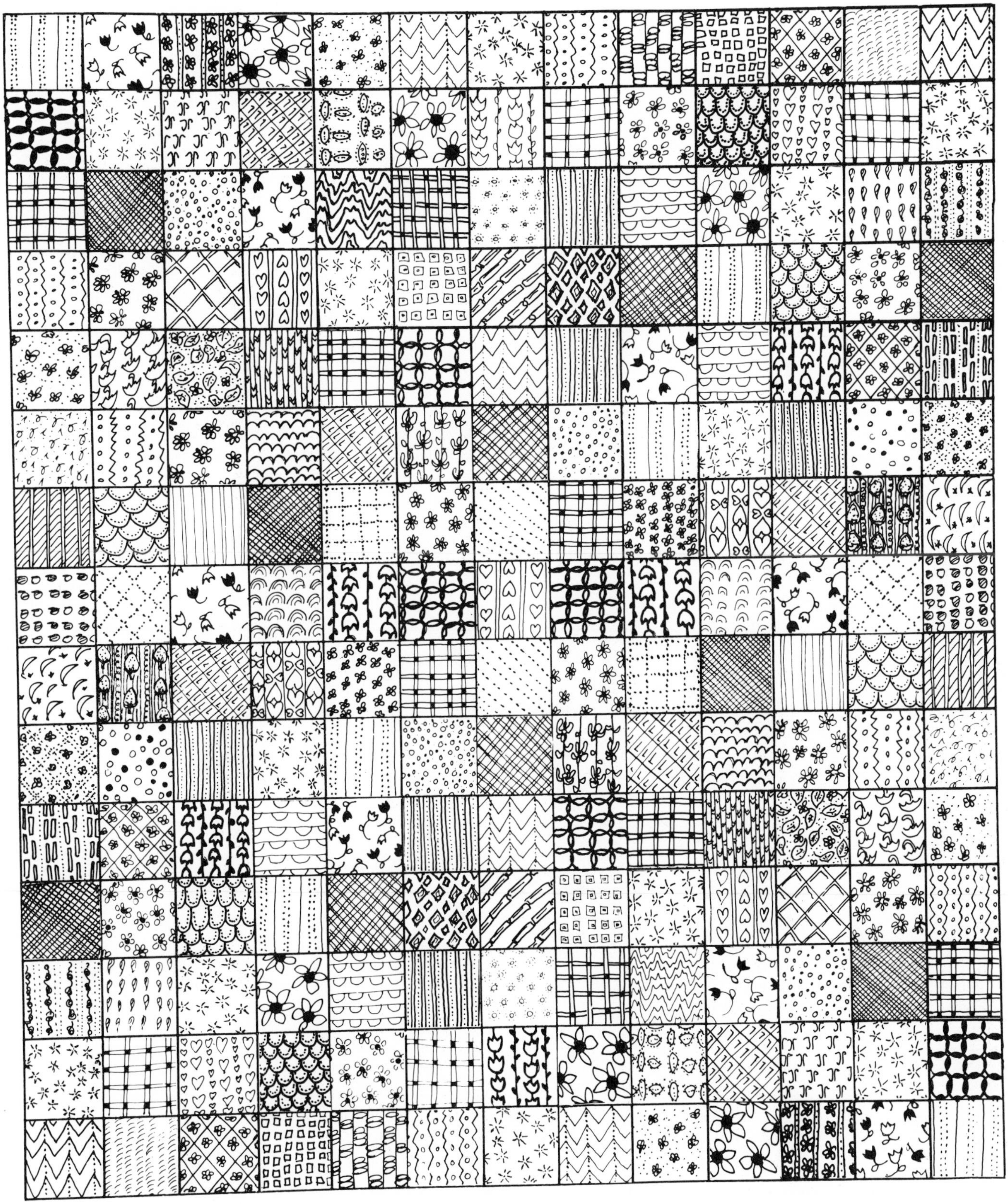

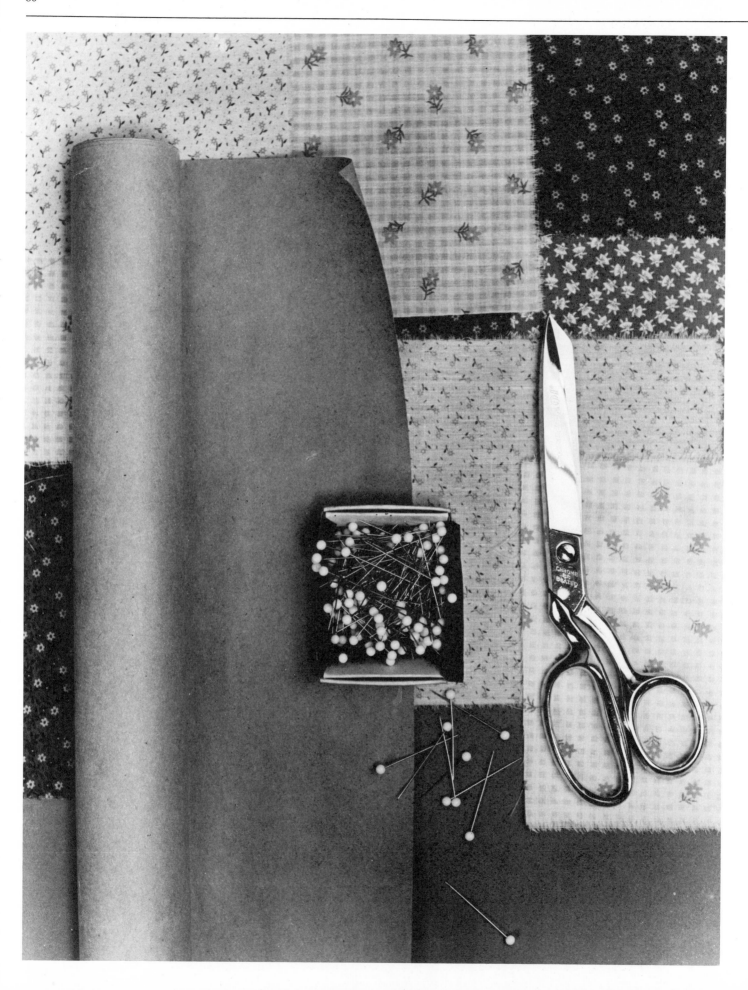

BROWN-PAPER-PATTERN METHOD

Many of my students feel most comfortable working in full scale (same size as the finished quilt). With my brown-paper-pattern method, individual patches are lain on a full-scale brown-paper pattern to form an original design. This design pattern serves as a guide, or kind of road map, which shows the order in which to assemble your quilt top.

Should you decide to use the brown-paper-pattern method, you will need patches to work with while laying out your design pattern. For complete instructions on cutting patches see Day I, *page 67.*

Start by joining two lengths of brown wrapping paper together with masking tape to form a larger paper pattern. Measure and cut the paper so that it is the same size as your finished quilt top. Should the quilt you are making be especially large, you may need to add another length of brown paper. Next, take your paper pattern and fold it in half and then in quarters. This will give you the exact center point.

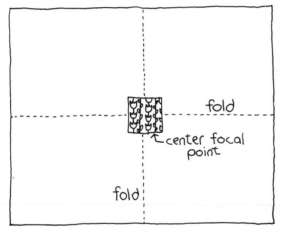

When working out the design on a brown-paper pattern, start with the center focal point.

Take your patches, which you have sorted according to color and pattern, and turn them right-side up. Look carefully through them and select the one with the pattern and color you like best. This is the patch you will use as the center focal point of your quilt top. Pin the center of this patch to the center of your paper pattern. Now place the second and third patches on each side of the center patch. This will create a "mirror image" which will be reflected throughout your paper pattern. Continue in this manner, working horizontally, vertically, and diagonally, filling in as you go, and always letting your eye return to your center focal point. As you pick up each patch to lay it on your brown-paper pattern, be careful to keep the lengthwise grain lines, marked on the wrong side of each patch (*see Day 2, page 73*), all going in the same direction. (This way, you will never have to turn patches as you pick them up to pin together.)

When laying out your patches, feel loose and free to experiment, stepping back occasionally to see your results. Remember, if you don't like the design pattern you have laid out, change it. On the other hand, don't overwork your design. Once you are satisfied, leave it alone. Your next quilt will be different.

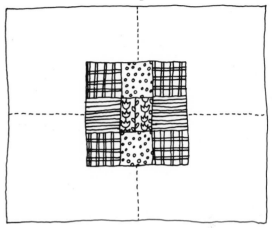

Laying out the brown-paper pattern.

In laying out your pattern try for an even distribution of light and dark colors, and a difference in scale between large and small patterns. To create a harmonious effect aim for a contrast of fabric patterns, which may be stripes, dots, checks, florals, and solid colors. When you have laid out all the patches to form a design, the number of rows and patches in the paper pattern should correspond with the information you wrote on your Quilt Fact Sheet.

Number the rows in your pattern as shown in the diagram. Starting with the center row, which is Row 1, then the row to the left of the center row (Row 2), and then the row to the right of center (Row 3). It may seem odd to number in this way, but this is actually the order in which you will join them. Continue until you have numbered all the rows.

Numbered rows on the brown-paper pattern.

Now you are ready to begin pinning your patches together. For directions see *Day 2, page 73.*

PASTE-UP-PATTERN METHOD

You should try my Paste-Up-Pattern Method if you are a person who enjoys working on a small scale. Apartment dwellers may find this method especially convenient. Since the method is small in scale, you can lay out your design pattern while sitting at your kitchen or dining room table.

Refer back to your Quilt Fact Sheet and see how many patches are to be cut and how many vertical and horizontal rows there are. That number of squares should be ruled in on your paper. Then take a 20- by 20-inch (51.20- by 51.20-cm.) sheet of any paper you have on hand and rule in 1- by 1-inch (2.56- by 2.56-cm.) squares, as shown. By using your C-Thru ruler as a guide, you can line its outer edge up with the edge of your paper and draw lines vertically, then horizontally. This will give you a design pattern of 1- by 1-inch squares quite easily.

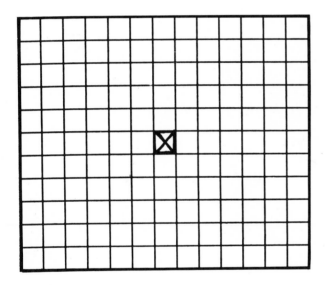

When laying out patches on a paste-up pattern, start at the center focal point.

Now cut out 1- by 1-inch patches of fabric in each of the colors and patterns you plan to use in your quilt top and work out a design that is pleasing to your eye. Paste these patches down with glue or rubber cement.

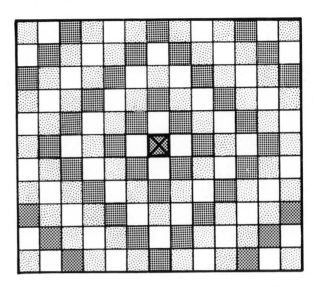

Fabric patches glued down on paste-up pattern.

Number your rows, as shown in the diagram, in order to keep track of the patches that you will later pin, sew, and press together. Then, using your paste-up pattern as a guide, cut out the same number of full-size 7- by 7-inch (17.92- by 17.92-cm.) patches in the fabrics you have pasted down. (See *Day I, page 67* to see how this is done.)

GRAPH-PAPER-PATTERN METHOD

If you have decided to use all solid-colored fabrics in your quilt top, then my Graph-Paper-Pattern Method is for you. By using the combination of graph paper and felt-tipped pens, you can create simple but imaginative designs.

In the back of the book you'll find several printed pages of graph paper. Detach a page and you will have a sheet of graph paper, saving you a trip to the store. Mark out the designated number of grids, each grid representing a patch as shown. How do you know how many patches to mark for? Go back and check your Quilt Fact Sheet dimensions for the number of rows in your quilt top. Then count off this number of squares on the graph paper.

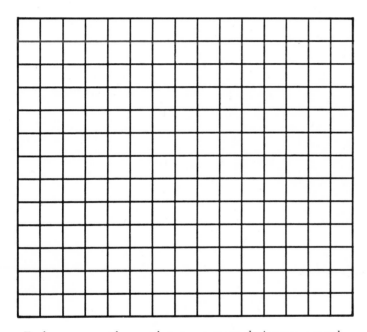

Each square on the graph-paper pattern designates a patch.

Using felt-tip pens or crayons in colors corresponding to those in the fabrics you have selected, create your design. Notice that you will have an odd number of rows.

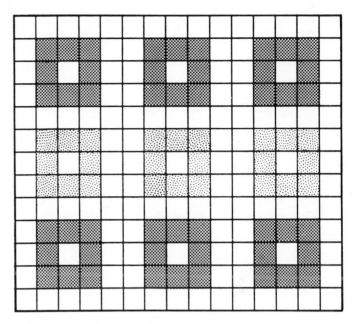

Colors marked in on graph-paper pattern.

Number your rows, as shown in the diagram, in order to keep track of the patches that you will later pin, sew, and press together. Then, using your graph-paper pattern as a guide, cut out one 7- by 7-inch (17.92- by 17.92-cm.) patch (in corresponding color) for each of the grids you have marked in.

Day
1

Today you will:
1. Rip off selvages.
2. Taking template, mark in fabric at 7-inch (17.92-cm.) intervals.
3. Clip and rip fabric into strips.
4. Pencil in lengthwise-grain lines and stack strips.

1 RIP OFF SELVAGES.

Many of my students ask, "What is the selvage, and where can it be found? What is its purpose, and why should it be removed?"

The selvage is the finished, woven edge found on each vertical side of a piece of fabric. The purpose of the selvage is to keep the newly woven piece of fabric from stretching as it passes through the various processes of dyeing, printing, and finishing.

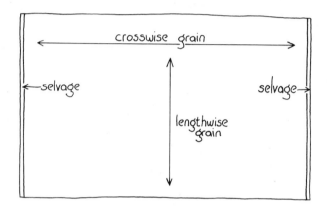

The lengthwise grain, crosswise grain, and selvages of a piece of fabric.

The selvage can help you by acting as a signal which indicates the lengthwise and crosswise grains of the fabric. The lengthwise grain runs parallel to the selvage. The crosswise grain runs from selvage to selvage. The warp threads are always the lengthwise threads. The weft threads are always the horizontal threads (sometimes called the "filler threads").

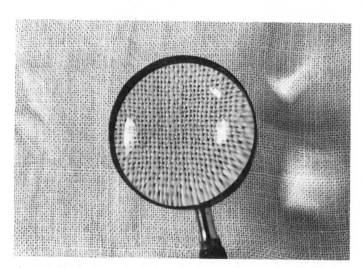

A magnified view of the lengthwise and crosswise grains of a piece of fabric.

When working with a piece of fabric, I find the quickest and simplest way to have uniform patches is to immediately establish the lengthwise grain of the fabric. This is done by first ripping off the selvages, by making a ½-inch (1.28-cm.) cut in on each side of the selvages, and then ripping these selvages off in a strong, swift downward motion.

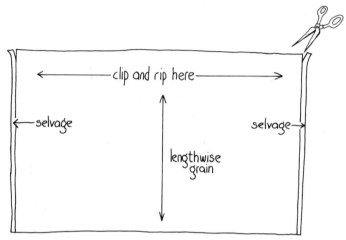

The selvage is clipped ½ inch in and ripped off in a strong and swift downward motion.

Ripping your fabric may seem like a very strange way of preparing it. No, you won't destroy your fabric by ripping. As a matter of fact, it's one of the simplest ways I know of to establish a straight edge along the lengthwise grain of a piece of fabric. Once you have ripped on the lengthwise grain, patches cut from these strips can't help but be straight.

Ripping off the selvage.

Being *on grain* (*see Glossary*) means your patches can be joined, sewn, and pressed together more easily. Later on, when you have finished your quilt top, it will lie smooth and flat without any ripples. Ripples can happen easily when your patches are *off grain* (*see Glossary*).

If you are using scraps of fabric too small to rip (if you are using leftover fabric scraps to make an American One-Patch Quilt, for example), take your template and trace around it. You will need enough fabric to cut multiples of two, four, six, eight, etc. If you have one scrap of fabric you simply love and you can only get one patch from it, use that patch as your center motif.

Since selvages will usually be cut off on small scraps of fabric, you can determine the lengthwise grain of an odd-shaped scrap by pulling the fabric vertically and horizontally. The crosswise grain is firm when pulled horizontally, while the lengthwise grain can be determined by its having a certain stretching quality.

Now, immediately, before you forget, pencil in a lengthwise-grain line. Place your template on top of the line you have just penciled in. Patches cut in this manner will always be on grain.

Note: Patches cut haphazardly will be off grain.

Your ripped-off selvages need not go to waste. Use them as strings for tying packages. They even make unusual and attractive gift ribbons, which children especially like.

2 TAKING TEMPLATE, MARK IN FABRIC AT 7-INCH (17.92-CM.) INTERVALS.

Now take your template and, placing it as shown and using a sharp #2 pencil, make a mark every 7 inches (17.92-cm.) (unless, of course, your template is a different size) along the crosswise grain of your fabric, moving your template as you mark.

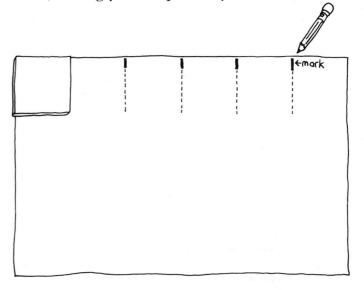

Move the template along the crosswise grain of the fabric and mark in patches at 7-inch intervals.

3 CLIP AND RIP FABRIC INTO STRIPS.

Clip in ½ inch (1.28 cm.) at each penciled-in line with scissors. Rip each strip in a strong, swift downward motion the length of your fabric, as shown.

The correct method of ripping fabric into strips. Always keep both arms close to the body and rip with a strong, downward motion.

An incorrect method of ripping fabric into strips. Note that the arm is thrust forward. This will stretch the fabric out of shape.

An incorrect method of ripping fabric into strips. Note that the arms are away from the body. This will stretch the ripped strips out of shape.

While ripping strips of fabric, you may discover that some ripped strips do not lie flat. It may be because of the differences in yarn weight, the way in which the fabric was woven, or the finishing-off process. Do not be alarmed. Merely pull the fabric back into shape and press flat with a steam iron.

If fabric has been stretched out of shape, pull back into shape diagonally.

When ripping strips of striped fabric first place fabric right side up. Rip one strip, then place this ripped strip, right side up, on top of the striped fabric, matching the stripes. Care must be taken to match stripes properly, otherwise stripes will repeat unevenly. Pin and cut out with scissors.

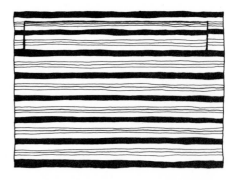

When ripping strips of striped fabric, place one ripped strip, right side up, on the fabric, being careful to match stripes, then pin and cut out with scissors.

4 PENCIL IN LENGTHWISE-GRAIN LINES AND STACK STRIPS.

After you have ripped your strips and pressed them flat on both sides, use a yardstick and pencil in a line down the center for the full length of each strip, as shown. Don't worry about centering this line exactly. It is there merely to indicate the lengthwise grain of your patches, once they have been cut.

Mark the lengthwise grain on ripped strips.

Line drawn on wrong side of strips to designate lengthwise grain.

Stack strips, one on top of another (wrong side up), according to color and pattern. Put them aside to be marked and cut into patches in Day 2.

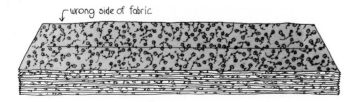

Ripped strips stacked one on top of the other, wrong side up.

DAY 1: CHECK YOUR WORK EACH DAY

Make sure you:
1. Rip selvages off fabrics.
2. Take template and mark in at 7-inch (17.92-cm.) intervals along the crosswise grain of fabric.
3. Rip strips in a strong, swift downward motion, rather than pulling or stretching fabric apart while ripping.
4. Straighten strips that are not lying straight by pulling and pressing them into shape.
5. Press strips flat on both sides, if necessary.
6. Pencil in a lengthwise-grain line on ripped strips.
7. Layer strips wrong side up in preparation for Day 2.

Day
2

Today you will:

1. Mark in patches with template and cut out patches with scissors.
2. Stack your patches.
3. Taking the windowpane template, mark in a ½-inch (1.28-cm.) seam allowance on patches.
4. Pin your first row together.

1 MARK IN PATCHES WITH TEMPLATE AND CUT OUT PATCHES WITH SCISSORS.

Make sure your ripped strips are stacked one on top of another (wrong side up), with no more than three strips in each pile, and make certain that the strips line up exactly and that the edges are perfectly aligned.

Take your template and mark in at 7-inch (17.92-cm.) intervals (or whatever size your template is) along the top strip in each pile with a sharp pencil, as shown. Make absolutely sure that your template is aligned straight on the ripped strips, as shown.

Pin in the center of each patch, as shown, and cut with sharp scissors through all three strips.

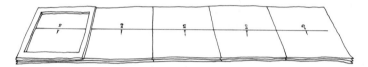

Mark in patches with template along the ripped strip.

When cutting your patches, never lift your scissors into the air. Keep them perpendicular to the table or ironing board (where I like to work), using your left hand as a weight. Cut in a long, sweeping motion.

When cutting out the patches, scissors should be perpendicular to the table.

Do not lift or chop at your fabric. Make sure that you cut on the straight pencil line that you have marked in.

2 STACK YOUR PATCHES.

As you cut, separate all patches into piles according to color and pattern, wrong side up. At this point, take care to align all outer edges evenly, and make certain that the lengthwise-grain lines that you penciled in earlier all go in the same direction.

Separate all patches into piles according to color and design. For each pile write the number of patches in that pile on a piece of paper and place the note on top of the pile.

In order to keep an accurate account of the number of patches you have already cut, place a note with the number of patches you have cut on each individual pile.

As already noted in the section on buying your fabric, you will be able to get thirty 7- by 7-inch (17.92- by 17.92-cm.) patches out of 1 yard of 45-inch

(1.15-m.) fabric, or twenty-five 7- by 7-inch patches out of 1 yard of 36-inch (92.16-cm.) fabric.

When using a one-way design (see *Glossary*), such as the cowboy motif shown in the photograph, the job is more expensive and time-consuming. But, while shopping, if you see a fabric with a one-way design that you would like to incorporate in your quilt top, unroll the fabric and check it carefully to see how often the one-way design repeats. If the design is spaced 6 to 10 inches (15.36 to 25.60 cm.) apart and you plan on repeating it often, you will need 1 or 2 yards (92.16 cm. or 1.84 m.) of extra fabric. Be sure not to scrimp; any leftover fabric can be used for future quilt-making projects.

To cut your one-way design each patch must be matched, pinned, and cut out separately. Cut out one patch first to use as a guide, place it on top of another motif, pin, and cut. Continue to cut out each motif separately until you have enough patches to lay out on your paper pattern.

When you unpin your patches, note that each patch has part of the lengthwise-grain line that you marked in earlier on each fabric strip. Each patch also has two raw edges and two straight edges. The two raw edges represent the lengthwise grain of the fabric (which you have ripped), while the two straight edges, which you have cut, represent the crosswise grain of the fabric.

I find that it is helpful if you stack the patches wrong side up. This way you can clearly see the lengthwise-grain lines marked in earlier. All the raw edges are going in one direction, and all the cut edges are going in the other direction.

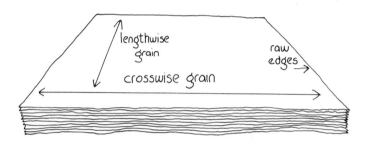

Stack patches wrong side up with all the raw edges perfectly aligned.

When cutting out a one-way design, each patch must be matched, pinned, and cut out separately.

Later, when you pick up your patches to form rows, it will be the cut edges that you first pin together. Be careful to keep these cut edges perfectly aligned, making certain that the lengthwise-grain line you penciled in earlier is running in the same direction on all patches. By keeping the lengthwise and crosswise grains of all your patches going in the same directions, you avoid future mistakes. (If lengthwise and crosswise grains are mixed, the patches will not join together as well.)

Although exceptions to this rule can be made, you should only do so if it is to improve your design pattern. For example, you might wish to change the direction of a stripe or a figure to create a more heightened visual effect. Only do this when absolutely necessary to your intrinsic design.

3 TAKING THE WINDOWPANE TEMPLATE, MARK IN A ½-INCH (1.28-CM.) SEAM ALLOWANCE ON PATCHES.

Taking your windowpane template (*see page 19*), lay it on the top patch of a stack of patches. Holding the windowpane template flat with one hand, use the other hand to mark in a line with a sharpened pencil all the way around the inner edge of the template. For this job it's best to hold the sharpened pencil at an angle. This way, the line that you are penciling in will be tight against the edge of your template, and, therefore, more exact. Continue in this manner, marking seam allowance on each patch. As you mark in the seam allowance, restack patches according to color and pattern.

Mark in seam allowance on patch.

Keep in mind that your marked-in seam allowance is your guide for sewing, so be as precise as possible while marking in your seam allowance lines. You will find it difficult to sew a straight line if the sewing line isn't precise, so double-check yourself.

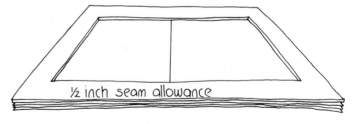

Windowpane template on a stack of patches ready to be marked in.

4 PIN YOUR FIRST ROW TOGETHER.

Now that you have stacked all of your patches, you may be anxious to see what one finished row looks like when it is pinned together. If you'd like to do this, check ahead to *Day 3, number 1.* This will give you an idea of what your quilt will eventually look like. Afterwards, hang the pinned row carefully on a pants hanger so that it will not wrinkle. On the other hand, you may decide that you've done enough work for Day 2 and prefer to wait until Day 3 to pin your first row together.

DAY 2: CHECK YOUR WORK EACH DAY

Make sure you:
1. Mark in patches with template.
2. When cutting your patches, never lift your scissors into the air. Always keep them perpendicular to the table.
3. Count patches as you work.
4. Stack patches wrong side up after cutting, with the lengthwise-grain lines all going in the same direction.
5. Mark in a ½-inch (1.28-cm.) seam allowance on wrong side of patches with windowpane template.
6. Draw in a straight seam allowance line on patches.
7. Pin first row of patches together.

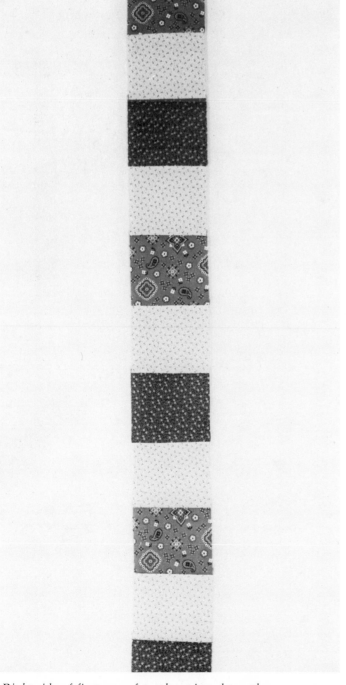

Right side of first row of patches pinned together.

Day 3

Today you will:

1. Pin patches together, using your design pattern as a guide.
2. Sew patches together and press as you go.
3. Sew vertical rows together and press as you go.

As you thumb through Day 3, it may seem like a killer day to you, but it's not. Notice the many illustrations that will help as you pin, sew, and press your rows of patches. Let me stress here that after you have pinned, sewn, and pressed the last row of your quilt top, you have literally finished making your quilt top.

With my 7-Day Method, you can finish a quilt top in one day, depending on the size of the quilt and the amount of time you have to devote to the making of it. However, if you have less time or are making an extra-large quilt, the work in Day 3 might well take you longer than a day. So, unless you're a speed demon, take your time and work at your own pace. There's no reason why you have to do it all in one day unless you want to.

1 PIN PATCHES TOGETHER, USING YOUR DESIGN PATTERN AS A GUIDE.

Now, using your design pattern as a guide, you are ready to assemble your quilt top. Regardless of which method you have used to plan your design—the brown-paper pattern, paste-up pattern, or graph-paper pattern—everything you see on one side of your quilt design should be reflected on the opposite side in each direction—horizontally, vertically, and diagonally. Seeing this mirror image provides you with a method of checking on yourself, row by row, while joining your rows of patches to form your quilt top.

Have you counted out your rows to make certain you know which is Row 1? Have you labeled it "Row 1," as shown? (If you have already pinned Row 1, on Day 2, then you can begin sewing it together. (*See Day 3, number 2.*)

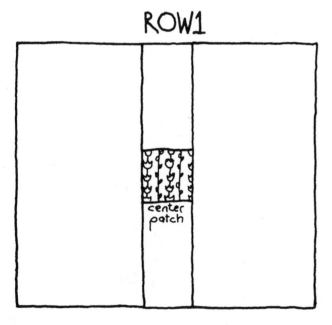

Mark in and label the center row, making certain you pick up the center patch first.

Before you pin patches together, make a mental note to begin picking up patches from the center of the shorter rows, starting with the center patch of the center row, as shown. You may ask, "Why am I working on the quilt sideways?" This is because the shorter rows are easier to handle when pinning and sewing them together. Now follow this procedure:

1. Pick up the center patch of Row 1 and the patch directly below it, placing the right sides together and aligning the cut edges.
2. Make certain that the vertical lines you marked in earlier on the wrong sides of your patches are running in the same direction.
3. Join these patches together by placing three pins at intervals, as shown.

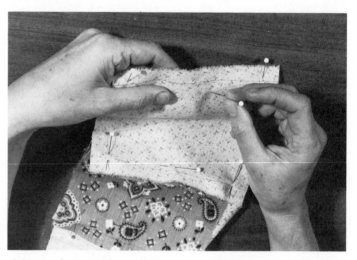

Join patches together, placing three pins at intervals shown.

Continue picking up the patches below the center in Row 1 and pinning them together edge to edge, right sides together. Then pick up the remaining patches in Row 1, above the center patch, checking yourself to make certain that the sequence of patterns is being repeated in reverse order above the center patch, as it is below. Do you see the mirror image? Pin these patches together, following the same procedure. Now you are ready to sew your patches together.

2 SEW PATCHES TOGETHER AND PRESS AS YOU GO.

Sewing your quilt together is the step that takes the longest period of time. Skilled persons who use a sewing machine may be able to whip their quilts up quickly. People who are making their quilts by hand may enjoy the leisure of slowly hand-sewing their quilts. Whatever method you are using, work at your own pace.

Sometimes, when we begin working with a friend, we may compare our own progress with that of our friend's. This is natural; everyone tends to do this. But it's better not to. Your friend may have more experience than you, and may work more quickly. Always consider your own priorities first. Then the time you spend in making your quilt will be both enjoyable and productive.

If you plan on sewing by machine, thread your sewing machine with cotton-covered polyester thread. Use a size 11 to 14 needle in your sewing machine (11 for lightweight fabric, 14 for medium-weight fabric). The size of the stich can be 8 to 10 stitches per inch (20 to 25 stitches per cm.). I find any stitch smaller than 10 to the inch difficult to rip out if a mistake has been made, while most stitches larger than 8 to the inch are too loose. Sew patches together horizontally with a ½-inch (1.28-cm.) seam allowance. Sew all the way from one outer edge to the other. Since machine sewing is strong enough, extra reinforcing is unnecessary.

If you don't own a sewing machine, this is a good time for you to practice and improve your hand-sewing. Simply thread a fine needle with a single thread. Cut the thread on a diagonal so that you can thread the needle more easily. Then sew patches together horizontally with a ½-inch (1.28-cm.) seam allowance, using a tiny running stitch, as shown.

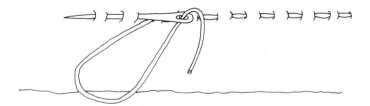

The running stitch.

Sew from right to left. Since knots wear out, I find it helpful to reinforce each seam for ½-inch (1.28 cm.) from the outer edge as you sew, as shown.

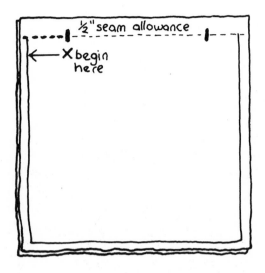

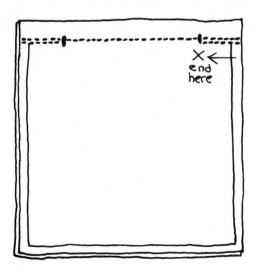

If sewing by hand, it is a good idea to reinforce each seam.

Remember, machine sewing may be fast, but hand sewing is just as strong and long-lasting.

Now that you are putting your quilt top together, I'd like to share with you my idea for making your work portable. I call my idea "Traveling Patches" which, when folded, are no longer than "half a sandwich."

Traveling patches folded like an accordion.

"Half Sandwiches" when folded are small enough to fit in a plastic sandwich bag, making them convenient to carry around.

"Traveling Patches" and "Half a Sandwich" probably sound like song titles to you. But the method serves as a very practical way of working while away from home. Here's how it's done:

Take a marked and pinned row of patches and fold the pinned edges together like an accordion. Then fold this row of patches in half, and it is no larger than half a sandwich.

When you visit friends or travel, take along your row of patches, a needle, thread, and a small nail or embroidery scissors. All of this is compact enough to fit into a plastic sandwich bag or small envelope. The whole thing takes up less room than a half-sandwich.

In any case, once you have finished sewing Row 1, remove all the pins and press the seams closed flat with a downward motion, as shown.

Press the seams of each row closed flat with a downward motion.

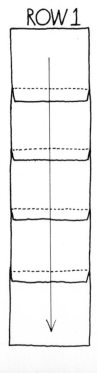

ROW 1

Row 1 seams pressed closed flat with a downward motion.

Press the right side of Row 1 perfectly flat.

Now turn the row that you have just pressed over and press the right side perfectly flat.

Don't squoosh your patches into a paper bag! After pressing your row of patches, don't crowd it into a brown paper bag so that it wrinkles. You may laugh, but some of my students actually come to class with their patches all mashed together. On the other hand, some students bring their patches to class in a gift box, carefully wrapped in tissue paper. You needn't go to that extreme either. I find it most efficient to pin my pressed rows of patches onto my brown-paper pattern (if that's what I've been using) as I go or to hang them on a pants hanger.

Now, starting at the top of Row 2 (to the left of Row 1), pick up, pin, and sew the entire row of patches, checking your pattern to make certain that the sequence of patches in Row 2 is the opposite of the sequence of patches in Row 3 (to the right of Row 1). After Row 2 is completed, press seams flat with an upward motion (the opposite of Row 1). Then press the right side of this row perfectly flat.

3 SEW VERTICAL ROWS TOGETHER AND PRESS AS YOU GO.

Join Row 2 to Row 1 by pinning at each junction point, making sure patches match, as shown. Sew Row 2 to Row 1 with a ½-inch (1.28-cm.) seam allowance along the length of your strip.

Pin Row 1 to Row 2, placing pins 1 inch in from edge.

Right side of Row 1 and Row 2 sewn together.

Here again, extreme caution must be taken that these junction points match exactly. When you begin picking up your patches, if you notice that one patch is slightly larger than another, don't try to stretch the smaller patch to fit the larger. Instead, try to fit the larger patch to the smaller by gently pressing in the excess fabric with your thumb, as shown in the photograph. This is called "easing in."

If one patch is slightly larger than another, ease it in while pinning.

Anchor the two patches together with pins placed in a vertical direction, so that the fabric you have eased in is gently gathered, but shows no puckering or pleats when sewn on the seam. (This is a very subtle movement, so handle with care.) Should the larger patch now look slightly gathered, do not be concerned. The batting in your quilt will later fill it out, and it will not be noticeable.

If there is too much excess fabric to be eased in, you may need to take out your horizontal seam, remark and resew it. Remember, if you are too far off in sewing your rows together, your quilt top will be crooked. But if you exercise extreme caution while sewing, your quilt top will be straight.

Now press the vertical seam you have just sewn between Row 1 and Row 2 closed flat toward the center, as shown. Then press the right side perfectly flat.

Repeat the same procedure with Row 3 and join it to the first two rows; press seam closed flat toward center, as shown. Then press right side perfectly flat.

Right side of Rows 1, 2, and 3 sewn together.

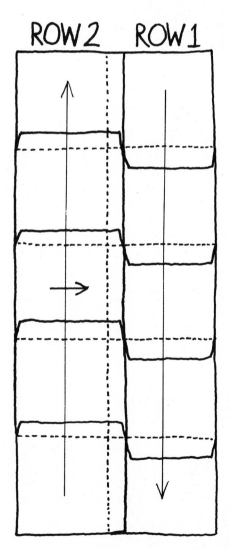

The seams of Row 2 are pressed closed upward and the seam connecting Rows 1 and 2 is pressed flat toward the center of the quilt (to the right).

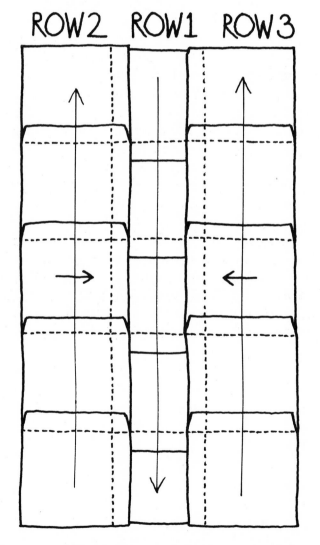

The seams of Row 3 are pressed closed upward and the seam connecting Rows 3 and 1 is pressed closed toward the center of the quilt top (to the left).

When you have completed your first three center rows, step back and look at your quilt. This is an exciting moment, because from here on you will literally begin to see your quilt grow before your eyes. I hope that you will be as inspired as most of my students are by this visual experience.

Continue to join your rows in this manner, alternating from left to right, until your quilt top is complete. As you can see, you are picking up, pinning, sewing, and pressing as you go. Once you have finished sewing and pressing your last row, you need never press your quilt top again.

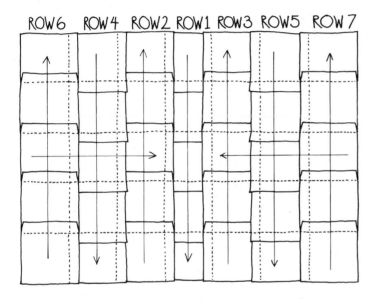

The back of the finished quilt top, showing in which direction to press seams.

Now that you've worked so hard, some of you may want to take a breather. Others may feel "high" from this experience. If so, this is the time to utilize this excess energy productively by working as quickly as possible to complete your quilt. In that case, go on to Day 4.

DAY 3: CHECK YOUR WORK EACH DAY

Make sure you:
1. Pick up rows of patches, making certain that the vertical lines you penciled in on the wrong side are all running in the same direction.
2. Pick up patches with right sides together and align cut edges perfectly to pin.
3. Pin 1 inch (2.56 cm.) in from cut edge.
4. Make certain to check that the sequence of patches is repeated as a mirror image throughout your design pattern.
5. Sew patches together, leaving a ½-inch (1.28-cm.) seam allowance.
6. Reinforce for a few stitches when hand-sewing patches together.
7. Press rows of patches on both sides.
8. Pin rows together carefully at each junction point before sewing rows together.
9. Sew all rows together with ½-inch (1.28-cm.) seam allowance.
10. Press all vertical seams on quilt top closed flat and toward the center on both sides.

Day

4

Today you will:

1. Measure your quilt top to learn how much backing fabric to buy.
2. Square off your quilt top with a yardstick.
3. Lay quilt top on top of batting and pin and baste into place.

1 MEASURE YOUR QUILT TOP TO LEARN HOW MUCH BACKING FABRIC TO BUY.

At this point, you may be getting anxious to finish your quilt. It's natural. Most of my students feel this way, too. Stop and relax a moment, though. You're almost home.

Take this breather to think about the color of your backing. It can be a solid-colored fabric, picking up one of the predominant colors in your quilt top, or it may be of a tiny calico pattern, picking up one of the calico patterns in your quilt top. As to the type of fabric, you can use poplin, broadcloth, or any smooth-textured cotton or Dacron-and-cotton fabric. (Some of my students like to use a colored percale bed sheet.)

This is not the time to scrimp on the amount of fabric you buy. Do use your measurements as a guide. However, I like to buy at least ½ yard (46.08 cm.) extra, just in case there is any discrepancy in the measuring or the fabric shrinks (a consideration if it is 100% cotton). Remember, if you have any scraps of fabric left over from your quilt-making, they can be used in the future for some smaller projects.

Measure the finished quilt top to find the correct size for backing, adding 4 inches to the length and width measurements.

To find the right size for your backing, measure your finished quilt top, adding 4 inches (10.24 cm.) to the length and 4 inches to the width to allow for your border. Now convert these dimensions to yards by dividing 36 into your quilt top dimensions. For most quilts you will have to piece two widths of backing fabric in the center with a ½-inch (1.28-cm.) seam allowance. If your quilt is especially large, you will have to piece three widths of fabric together. Remember to enter the backing measurements on your Quilt Fact Sheet.

Pin your backing fabric pieces right sides together, selvage to selvage. Then take your C-Thru ruler and, with a sharp pencil line, mark in a ½-inch (1.28-cm.) seam allowance the full length of your seam. *Do not remove the selvage.* Clip selvage ¼ inch (0.64 cm.) in on the diagonal (to keep seam flat and from pulling) every 10 inches (25.60 cm.). Press seam open flat, as shown.

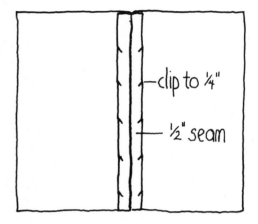

The seam of the backing fabric is clipped to ¼ inch to keep seam flat and to keep it from pulling.

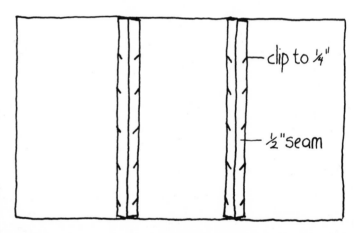

For large quilts you may have to join more than two pieces of backing fabric.

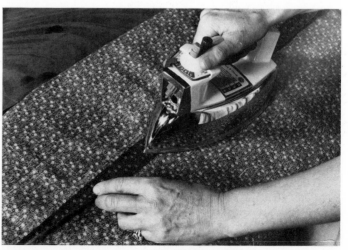

Press the seams of the backing fabric open flat.

2 SQUARE OFF YOUR QUILT TOP WITH A YARDSTICK.

To square off your quilt top is to straighten all the outer edges that may be slightly off. This can be due to irregularities in marking, cutting, or sewing. When you have finished your quilt top, a good way of telling whether or not your quilt top is straight is by laying it along any straight edge, such as a table or the boards of a parquet floor. If there are slight discrepancies, this is the time to make changes, because if the outer edges of your quilt are not straight, it will never look straight while lying on the bed.

Many of my students are confused when I tell them that they can square off a quilt top that is not straight to begin with. This is done by straightening the outer edges of your quilt top, which will give the entire quilt top the *illusion* of being straight. Lay a yardstick at right angles to a straight edge (such as the edge of a table). This creates a T-square. Then align the edge of the yardstick with the shortest patch along the outer edge of the quilt top and draw in a pencil line to the corner, as shown. Hold the pencil tightly (to

keep the point from breaking off) against the edge of the yardstick. If you can't see a pencil mark, use a fine felt-tipped pen. If your quilt is dark, use a white pencil. It will show up better than any other kind of marking. Then cut off any excess fabric outside your marked pencil lines.

Staying in the same position, turn the quilt top clockwise to you and realign the straightened cut edge of the quilt with the straight edge of the table. Lay your yardstick at right angles to the straight edge of your quilt top. Draw in a line, using your yardstick as a guide, and cut off any excess fabric, as before. Continue in this manner, straightening all the outer edges of your quilt top.

Many students ask me, "How can you know that this line will be straight?" Remember, this is an illusionary line you are creating. If your quilt has been sewn crooked, it can *never* actually be straight, but by using my squaring-off method, you will create the illusion that your quilt is straight.

Continue in this manner, "straightening" all the outer edges of your quilt top. Then cut off any excess fabric outside your marked pencil lines.

Square off the quilt top.

3 LAY QUILT TOP ON TOP OF BATTING AND PIN AND BASTE INTO PLACE.

What do modern quilt-makers use as batting for their quilts?

I find that a synthetic material, such as a bonded polyester, works best for me. It comes in sheets which are easy to lay out.

Fill in the batting size on your Quilt Fact Sheet. Batting is usually cut the same size as your finished quilt top, but, if you want your quilt to be larger than its original size, this is then the time to add a wider border to your quilt. This can be done by cutting your batting larger on all four sides. As an example, if you wish your border to finish off at 2½ inches (6.40 cm.), you would measure out 2 inches (5.12 cm.) from the edge of your finished quilt top all around, then mark in a line on the batting with felt-tip pen. Cut all the way around on this marked-in line. Make certain you allow for this wider border by adding 2½ inches (6.40 cm.) to the length and width of your finished backing dimensions. Also, make sure that you add this extra dimension to your length and width when measuring your quilt top to determine batting size.

For a wider border allow more batting.

In any case, lay your batting out on a flat surface, such as a hard wood floor or large table. Place patch-work top, face up, over batting. Pin patchwork and batting layers together from the *center* outward, smoothing down batting with the side of your hand as you work. Try to use pins that are extra long—1¼ inches (3.20 cm.). They work better for pinning the thicknesses of your quilt together.

Baste the batting and quilt top together.

At this point, it is quite natural for you to be anxious to complete your quilt. But this is the most crucial period of all, and if you rush ahead, without carefully following all of the necessary basting steps, you may run into problems. Basting is necessary because it securely anchors the layers of your quilt together without lumps, wrinkles, and bulges. For added protection, don't remove any bastings until your quilt is finished.

After pinning, baste the top layers to the batting horizontally and vertically, as shown, with basting stitches 8 to 10 inches (20.48 to 25.60 cm.) long. Then baste along outer edge of quilt with ½-inch (1.28-cm.) bastings sewn ½-inch in from outer edges. I find using a long needle and a long single thread helpful for basting quilt layers together.

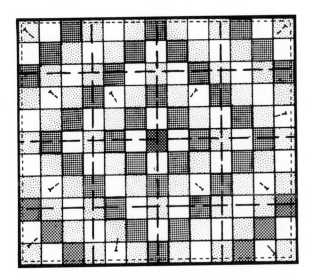

The quilt top is attached to the batting with basting stitches around the edges and up and down the rows.

Make absolutely certain that top and batting lie perfectly flat. Turn the two layers over so that the batting is on top and you are ready for the next day's work.

DAY 4: CHECK YOUR WORK EACH DAY

Make sure you:
1. Sew backing pieces together with a ½-inch (1.28-cm.) seam allowance and clip selvage edge in every 10 inches (25.60 cm.).
2. Press backing seam open flat.
3. Square off quilt top by marking in a straight, clear line with a yardstick.
4. Cut off excess fabric from quilt top outside marked pencil lines.
5. Cut batting for border larger, if you want your quilt to be larger.
6. Pin top to batting smoothly.
7. Baste top to batting.

Day
5

Today you will:
1. Mark center of batting.
2. Lay backing fabric over batting.
3. Baste three layers of quilt together around outer edges.

1 MARK CENTER OF BATTING.

Take your quilt and fold it in half lengthwise, with the batting side out. Place a pin mark lengthwise at each end of the fold. These pin marks will indicate the center of your quilt, as shown, when you unfold the quilt.

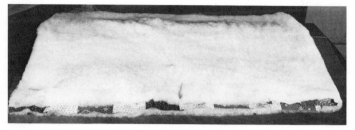

Fold quilt in half lengthwise, batting side out.

Pin marks designating center of quilt.

2 LAY BACKING FABRIC OVER BATTING, PIN, AND BASTE.

Take backing fabric and fold it in half, right sides together. Then lay folded edge along the pin marks of the quilt batting. Unfold, and pin backing to batting and quilt top, smoothing down backing with your hand as you pin. Then baste the three layers together horizontally and vertically, as shown.

Baste backing to quilt top and batting.

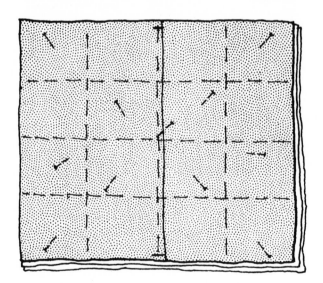

Backing pinned and basted to batting and quilt top.

3 BASTE THREE LAYERS OF QUILT TOGETHER AROUND OUTER EDGE.

Baste layers together around the outer edge, 1 inch (2.56 cm.) in as shown. Remove pins only after you have completed all of your bastings.

Turn layers over so that the quilt top is again on top, as shown and stop work for the day.

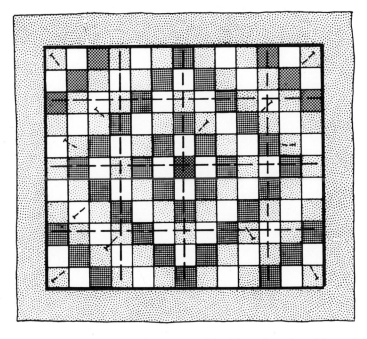

Right side of quilt top, batting, and backing pinned and basted together.

DAY 5: CHECK YOUR WORK EACH DAY

Make sure you:
1. Mark center of batting.
2. Lay backing on center of batting.
3. Pin and baste backing fabric to batting and quilt top.
4. Baste all three quilt layers together 1 inch (2.56 cm.) in from outer edge.
5. Turn basted quilt over so that quilt top now faces up.

Day 6

Today you will:
1. Measure your border.
2. Miter your corners.
3. Hand-sew border to quilt top.

1 MEASURE YOUR BORDER.

Take your C-Thru ruler and measure out 2 inches (5.12 cm.) from the edge of the quilt top all the way around. Mark in these 2 inches with a sharp pencil line on the backing fabric. Then cut off any excess backing fabric, leaving a 2-inch border. Fold this border in half, and then fold it over again onto the patchwork quilt top to form a 1-inch (2.56-cm.) border. This 1-inch border will greatly enhance your quilt and is similar to the frame for a painting. Make sure that the cut edge of the border fabric is tucked securely under the quilt top and batting.

Turn down the border and pin it to quilt top.

Then pin and smooth border into place, working from the center outward on each side. Leave about 5 inches (12.80 cm.) of border fabric free at each corner in order to simplify folding in your mitered corners.

2 MITER YOUR CORNERS.

Miter corners by folding fabric under at the inward corner at a 45-degree angle. After mitering the first corner, stay in the same position and rotate your quilt to bring each of the remaining corners into place for mitering. (It is much easier for you to move the quilt to you than it is for you to move around the quilt.) Do not overhandle or overpin your mitered corners; one pin is enough to hold your corner securely in place.

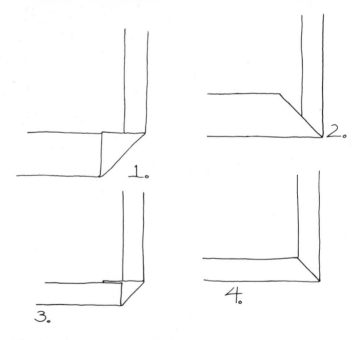

Miter corners of the quilt border.

The four basic steps to mitering corners.

Baste all the way around the border, 1/16 inch (0.16 cm.) in from the cut edge, using a ½-inch (1.28-cm.) basting stitch, as shown.

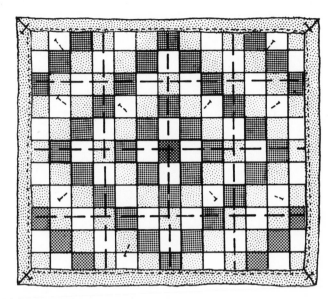

Basting around the quilt border.

3 HAND-SEW BORDER TO QUILT TOP.

The slip stitch is used to sew the folded edge of the border to the quilt top. First, slip the needle into the border at an angle, picking up just a thread or two just behind the fold, as shown. Then slip the needle at an angle into the border, as close as possible to where you have just entered. Take another slip stitch into the fold and continue on in this manner, making certain that each stitch is as concealed as possible. Do not remove pins and bastings until quilt is entirely finished.

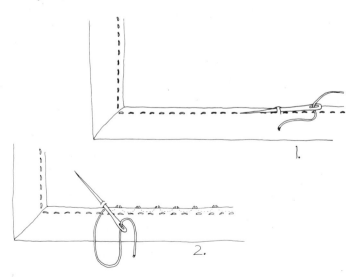

The three steps to making a slip stitch.

DAY 6: CHECK YOUR WORK EACH DAY

Make sure you:
1. Measure 2 inches (5.12 cm.) out from edge of quilt top and mark this line in on backing fabric.
2. Fold edge of backing in half to form 1-inch (2.56-cm.) border.
3. When folding in half, make certain that cut edges of backing are securely tucked under quilt top.
4. Pin and smooth border from center outwards.
5. Miter quilt corners by turning them inwards at a 45-degree angle.
6. Baste border 1/16 of an inch (0.16 cm.) in from outer edge.
7. When hand-sewing border, try to make your stitches as small as possible.

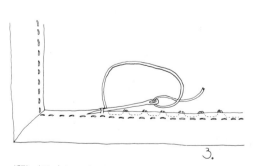

NOTE: dotted line indicates stitch slipped through fold.

Day 7

Today you will:

1. Learn to tuft.
2. Learn to quilt.
3. Write in and embroider your signature on your quilt.

When you have finished your quilt, I recommend tufting as the quickest and simplest way to hold the three layers of your quilt together. I don't recommend quilting for your first quilt, because it takes ten times longer to quilt than it does to tuft. Quilting also requires patience and experience in hand-sewing. However, many people would like to experiment with quilting right away. For those people, I am giving detailed instructions as to how this can be done.

1 LEARN TO TUFT.

Now you will secure the three layers of your quilt together by making a tufting stitch at the corners of each patch, as shown.

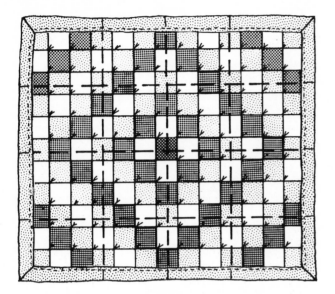

Tuft at the corners of each patch.

For tufting you can use silk floss, but it's not very durable. Wool thread can be attractive, but square knots tend to slip out. I find that Knit-Cro-Sheen works best for me, because it's the strongest and longest-lasting thread and holds a square knot best of all the others.

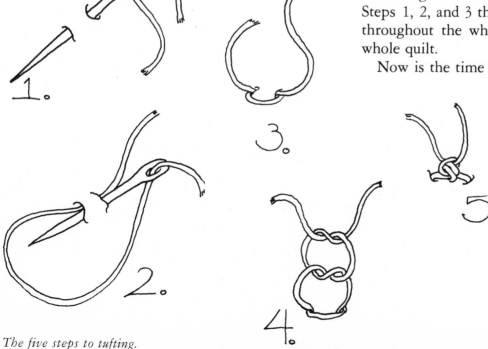

The five steps to tufting.

To tuft, thread a large-eyed embroidery needle with Knit-Cro-Sheen thread. Then follow these steps, as shown.

1. Make a stitch ⅛ inch (0.32 cm.) in length through all three thicknesses of the quilt.
2. Draw thread through stitch until about 2 inches (5.12 cm.) remains.
3. Make a backstitch in the identical place as the first stitch, and draw the thread through firmly, but without puckering the material.
4. Tie the ends of the thread together firmly with a square knot (right over left and left over right).
5. Make the knot firm and cut off both ends of the thread so that they are the same length, about 1/3 inch (0.85 cm.).

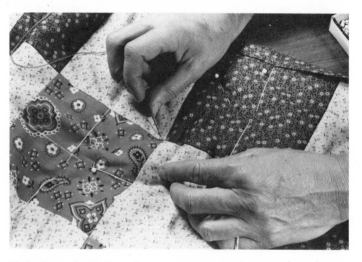

Tuft through all three layers of the quilt.

Tufting should be done in three separate stages: Steps 1, 2, and 3 throughout the whole quilt; Step 4 throughout the whole quilt; Step 5 throughout the whole quilt.

Now is the time to remove all pins and bastings.

2 LEARN TO QUILT.

Many people are fascinated by quilting. The mystery seems to be when and how it is done. This should not be a mystery to you, though, because you have learned that quilting is simply a way of anchoring the three layers of your quilt together by tiny running stitches.

A good way to learn how quilting is done is to practice the running stitch. Take a 7- by 7-inch (17.92- by 17.92-cm.) square of fabric left over from your quilt top and lay this onto a square of batting. Then lay these two layers onto a square piece of backing fabric. Pin and baste these three layers together and you have a miniature quilt to practice on. Draw three vertical and three horizontal lines every 2 inches (5.12 cm.) and quilt on these lines.

Take a small quilting needle, 1 inch (2.56 cm.) long, and thread it with quilting thread, about 12 inches (30.72 cm.) long. This thread has a silicon coating that enables it to slip through the three layers more easily, and it's stronger, too. Make a small knot at the end of your thread and pull through the top layer. Your knot will disappear and you will hear a tiny popping sound. This is called "popping your knot." Then, holding your miniature quilt in your hand, take tiny running stitches in the following way.

Make the first stitch on the line by pointing the needle towards the line and piercing the fabric with the needle point. Then, using your thimble, push the needle through three layers in an under-and-over motion. This will produce tiny running stitches. After you have quilted for a couple of inches, turn your work over. You will notice that the under stitches look only half the length of the upper stitches.

While quilting, aim for evenly made stitches, and be sure to wear your thimble. Otherwise, you may wear a hole in the center of your middle finger.

If you would like further practice before actually doing the running stitch on your quilt, you can make a pillow, as shown in *Gallery of Quilts*, and quilt around the inside of each square ½ inch (1.28 cm.) in from the edge. Whenever you decide to practice your quilting, remember to aim for smaller stitches and ones that are more uniform in size.

Once you have had some practice and feel more confident you may want to start quilting on your quilt. Remember, if you decide to do this, it may take four to six months, depending on how fast you work. If your quilt is small, you may feel comfortable holding it on your lap, starting in the center and working outward. A much larger quilt will have to be placed on a quilting frame (which can be bought inexpensively from Sears Roebuck or Montgomery Ward through their catalogs). Be sure not to remove any of your bastings before the quilt is finished.

3 WRITE IN AND EMBROIDER YOUR SIGNATURE ON YOUR QUILT.

Now that you have finished off your quilt, you might want to embroider your name on the border. This will serve the useful purpose of identifying you as the maker, the day the quilt was completed, and where it was made for posterity's sake. For example:

Made by Josephine Rogers on February 18, 1978, New York City.

If the quilt is being given as a gift, you might embroider, for example:

Made for Barbara Nolan by Josephine Rogers on June 1, 1978, New York City.

If you are making the quilt to give as a wedding gift, you might embroider, for example:

Made for the wedding of Judy Gibson and Bill Swiggard by Josephine Rogers on June 10, 1978.

I like to use a #2 pencil for writing on a lighter-colored border or a white pencil for writing on darker fabrics. Write out your name, date, and the place where your quilt was made. After you have written in your signature, try to embroider it right away. Otherwise, the pencil lines may lighten or rub away.

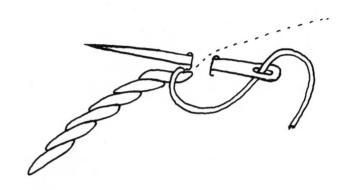

The outline stitch.

Select a color of embroidery floss that shows up on the border of your quilt. Now take an embroidery needle and thread it with two strands of embroidery floss. You will be making the outline stitch, as shown.

Working from left to right, take regular, slightly slanted stitches along the lines. The thread always emerges to the left side of the previous stitch.

When you have finished embroidering your signature, you are truly finished with your quilt. (The quilt shown in the photographs throughout this book is seen completed in the Gallery of Quilts.) Now call in the neighborhood and let them admire your work!

DAY 7: CHECK YOUR WORK EACH DAY

Make sure you:
1. Do not pull the stitches too tight while tufting.
2. Use a thimble if quilting—otherwise you will wear a little hole in your middle finger.
3. Try using a small needle for embroidering your name on your quilt. Remember, the smaller the needle, the smaller the stitch.
4. Separate your two strands of embroidery floss from the cut edge of your thread. This way, your thread will never snarl or knot.

Personalize the quilt by embroidering your name.

Care and Maintenance of Your Quilt

Using your quilt as a bedspread can revolutionize your daily bed-making. You need only roll out of bed, smooth your bottom and top sheets, and then, with a few quick, deft strokes of the hand, tuck your quilt into place. Your bed is made! (Make certain that you do use a top sheet, otherwise the borders of your quilt will soil faster than the rest of your quilt.)

Pillows can be tucked under, or you can stand them upright against the headboard. Or you may prefer to put your pillows away and, instead, use a small grouping of patchwork pillows made from the leftover quilt scraps.

Your quilt is strong, and, with normal wear and tear, it should last a long time. But if your children use it as a trampoline or your pets make it their favorite hangout, your quilt will soil and wear.

Under normal conditions your quilt need only be washed about once a year. With hard wear, your quilt will need to be washed much more often, and, as a result, will wear out more quickly.

I like to wash my quilt early in the morning on a clear, sunny day. Then it will have plenty of time to dry. To wash, take the quilt and carefully place it in the washing machine, using cool water. Add a mild detergent, such as Woolite, and set at the gentlest cycle for 10 to 15 minutes only. Remove gently and place the quilt in a clothes basket. Hang outdoors, if possible, backing side up, on a double or triple line to allow air to circulate around the quilt and to distribute the weight evenly. If you have a grass lawn, place the quilt, backing side up, on an old sheet or mattress cover. Turn several times during the day to allow air to circulate. If it's getting late and damp, place the quilt on the clothesline carefully to complete drying.

An electric clothes dryer can be used, but it will definitely shorten the life of your quilt. Dry-cleaning can be done, too, but pick a reliable cleaner who cleans on the premises. Make sure he has had experience with fine fabrics. Take the quilt to him in the morning, when the cleaning solvents are fresh, and ask him to clean it in his first cycle. That way, you're sure it will actually come out cleaner than when you brought it in.

As you can see, quilts are easy to care for, and, if cared for properly, your quilt will bring you many years of pleasure, warmth, and comfort.

When the weather gets too hot to use your quilt as a bedcover, it is time you stored it away for the summer.

The best place to store your quilt is in a cedar chest. If you don't own one, simply fold and store it on a shelf, uncovered, in a dry, dark closet. There is no need for mothballs, because moths do not attack products made of cotton.

Should you be concerned about protecting your quilt from dust, you can use a pillow case as a lightweight, porous slipcover. I don't recommend putting your quilt into a plastic bag. Allowing air to circulate freely is healthier for a product made mostly of natural fibers.

Hanging a quilt is just about the worst way to preserve it, since the weight of the quilt itself weakens all the fibers. But if you would still like to hang a quilt your child has outgrown or one that you no longer use on a bed, a simple way to do this is to add 1-inch (2.56-cm.) loops across the top of the quilt, approximately every 6 inches (15.36 cm.) from one outer edge to the other.

But the very best way is to buy 2-by-4s and build a frame the same size as the finished quilt. Then stretch and tack unbleached muslin in place on the frame. Place your quilt on top and tack it to the muslin base, using pins placed at an angle, every 7 inches (17.92 cm.), on the under edge of the quilt, where they will be invisible to the eye.

What's Next?

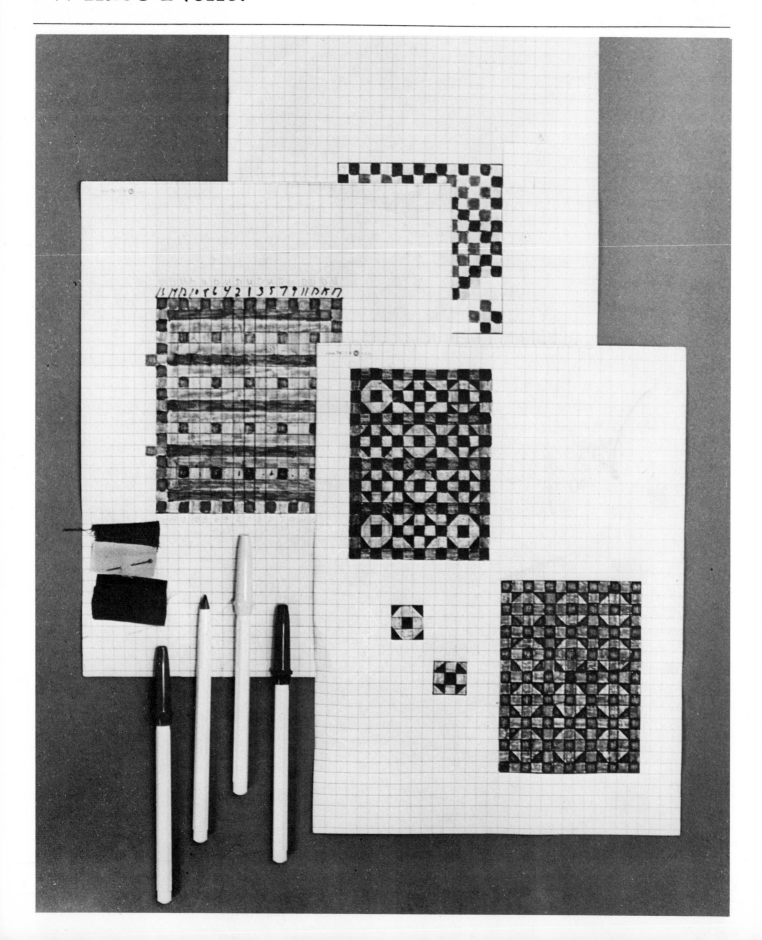

After finishing the last chapter, I just couldn't leave you with that burning question in your mind of "what's next?"

Yes, there are other things you can make in this book (see color) and I hope you will try them. But now that you've finished your first quilt, you may want to move on to a design pattern that is just a little more complex.

What I have done in this section is taken the American One-Patch Quilt and cut each patch in half, using only a light and a dark solid-colored fabric to form the design pattern shown. Should you like to redesign this quilt, you can change the whole look of the design pattern by using a small floral print combined with a solid-colored fabric.

The quilt measures 6½ feet wide by 7 feet long (2 m. by 2.15 m.). If you would like to make your quilt smaller, make your templates smaller—6 by 6 inches (15.36 by 15.36 cm.) instead of 7 by 7 inches (17.92 by 17.92 cm.).

The quilt has 230 pieces in all—forty-two dark squares and forty-eight dark triangles and ninety-two light squares and forty-eight light triangles. You will need 3 yards (2.76 m.) of dark fabric and 4 yards (3.68 m.) of light fabric.

The Stop Sign *floral block.*

The Stop Sign *quilt.*

To make your templates measure and cut out two 7- by 7-inch (17.92- by 17.92-cm.) squares. (One will be used for the square shapes and one for the triangular shapes.) Now take one square and draw a line diagonally from one inner corner to another to form a triangle. Add a ½-inch (1.28 cm.) seam allowance *only* to the line you have just drawn. Cut out precisely on the penciled-in line. Glue the square and triangular-shaped patterns to heavy cardboard.

Draw in a diagonal line on one template.

Measure out template on graph paper.

Cut out triangular template.

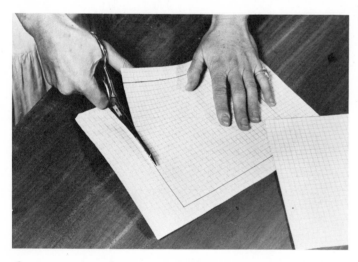

Cut out two templates.

Glue templates to cardboard.

Place these templates flat, right side down and weighted with a couple of telephone books on top, so they will dry without curling. Now you have two templates to use for cutting your square and triangular pieces.

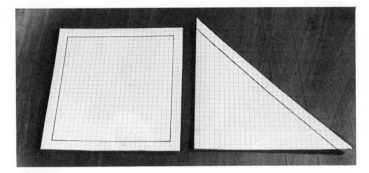

Finished square and triangular templates.

Take your template and trace around it on fabric, making certain to keep shapes as close together as possible so as not to waste fabric.

Place template on fabric and trace around it.

Count, stack pieces, and mark in a ½-inch (1.28-cm.) seam allowance with your C-Thru ruler as you go.

This simply pieced quilt is made in exactly the same method that you followed for your first quilt, using a ½-inch (1.28-cm.) seam allowance throughout. (See *Day 3*).

For finishing off your quilt, you might like to make a border, as shown on *page 96*. This quilt can make a striking wall hanging, if you have the wall space.

To hang the quilt, you will need to sew loops to the back of the quilt at the top, in order to suspend it from a rod.

After you have finished your quilt, you will notice that the all-over design forms individual blocks. (See *Glossary*.) These blocks can be used individually to make a pillow, shoulder bag, or baby quilt.

Piece in exactly the same way as you have just done in making your *7-Day Quilt*. The differences are that here, on every other vertical row, you must first join the triangles together before sewing them into rows. As you work, press all seams flat toward the center.

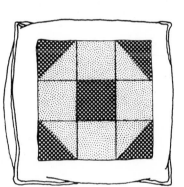

The Stop Sign *pillow.*

The Stop Sign *shoulder bag.*

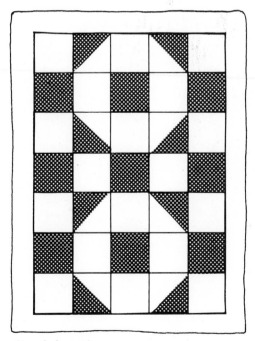

The Stop Sign *baby quilt.*

I hope that my book has whetted your appetite for the richness of this craft, and that some of you will feel inspired to taste further. If that should happen, I'm glad, because that is what the *7-Day Quilt* book is all about.

Cut-Out Templates

DETACH THIS PAGE TO MAKE A
TEMPLATE FOR MARKING PATCHES
AND SEAM ALLOWANCE

Materials needed:
1. 10- by 10-inch (25.60- by 25.60-cm.) piece of heavy cardboard
2. Carter's Rubber Cement or Elmer's Glue

A Cut along this line

B Patch marking line

½" seam allowance

C Seam allowance line

After you have detached this page and cut along line A, paste this entire section to a piece of heavy cardboard. Use rubber cement or white glue and make sure cement covers the entire surface so there are no loose edges to come unglued. Dry template on flat surface, right side down; place several phone books on top of it so it will be perfectly flat when dry.

Using your ruler held firmly on Line B, cut carefully along this line. You now have a 7-inch-square (17.92-cm.-sq.) template to mark your patches for cutting. This template is used, as is, in Day 1.

Holding your ruler firmly on Line C, and, using a single-edge razor blade, carefully cut along this line and remove the inner section of the template. When you lay this "windowpane" template down on a patch you have cut and trace around the inside of the template, it will automatically give you a ½-inch (1.28-cm.) seam allowance.

A second page similar to this one follows, in case your first effort has not been perfectly accurate. Then, you will see several other pages with smaller templates—5-inch, 6-inch, 3-inch, and 4-inch (12.8-cm., 15.36-cm., 7-68-cm., and 10.24-cm.)—for smaller-sized patches.

C Seam allowance line

½" seam allowance

B Patch marking line

7-Inch-Square Template

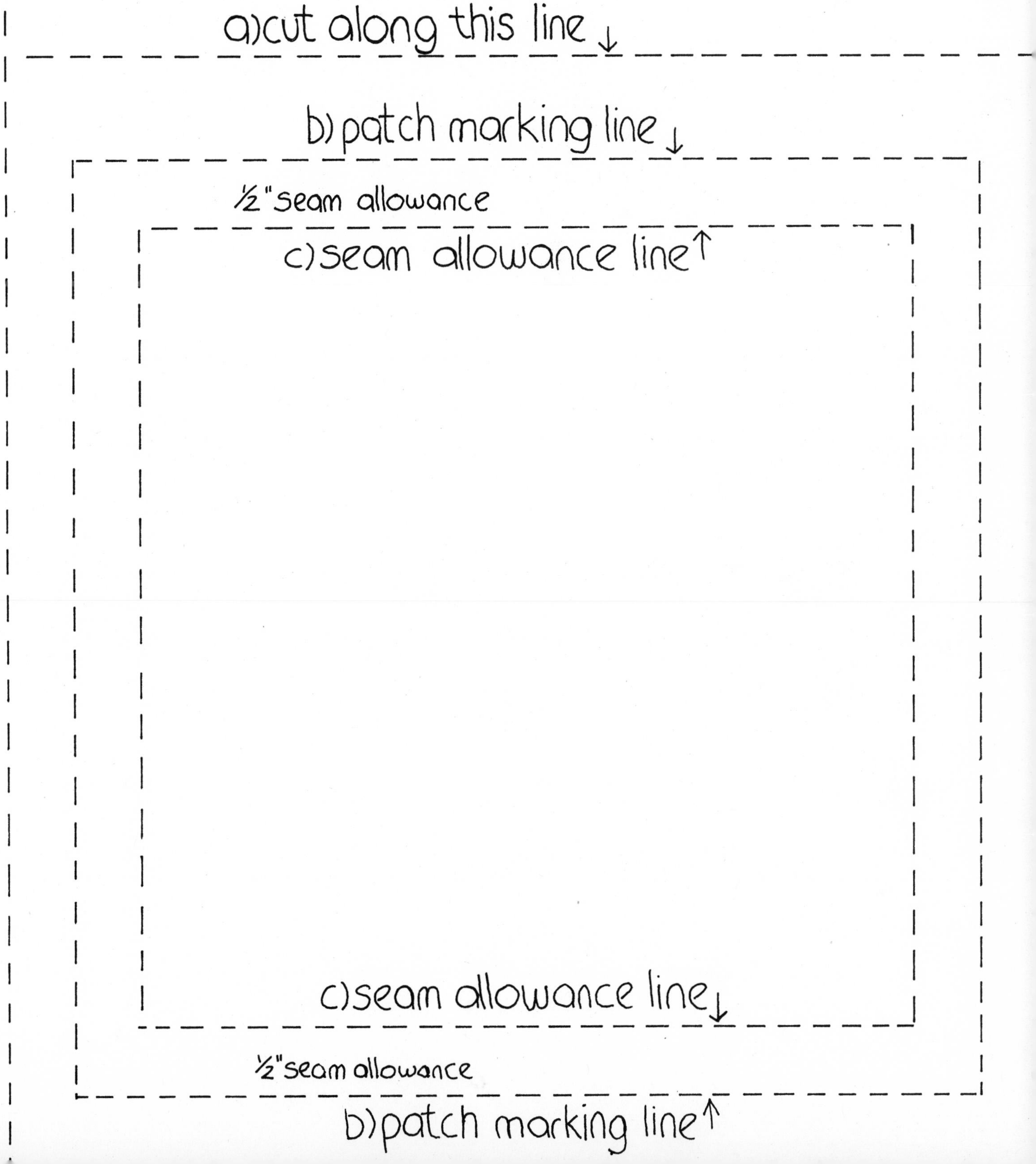

a) cut along this line ↓

b) patch marking line ↓

½" seam allowance

c) seam allowance line ↑

c) seam allowance line ↓

½" seam allowance

b) patch marking line ↑

6-Inch-Square Template

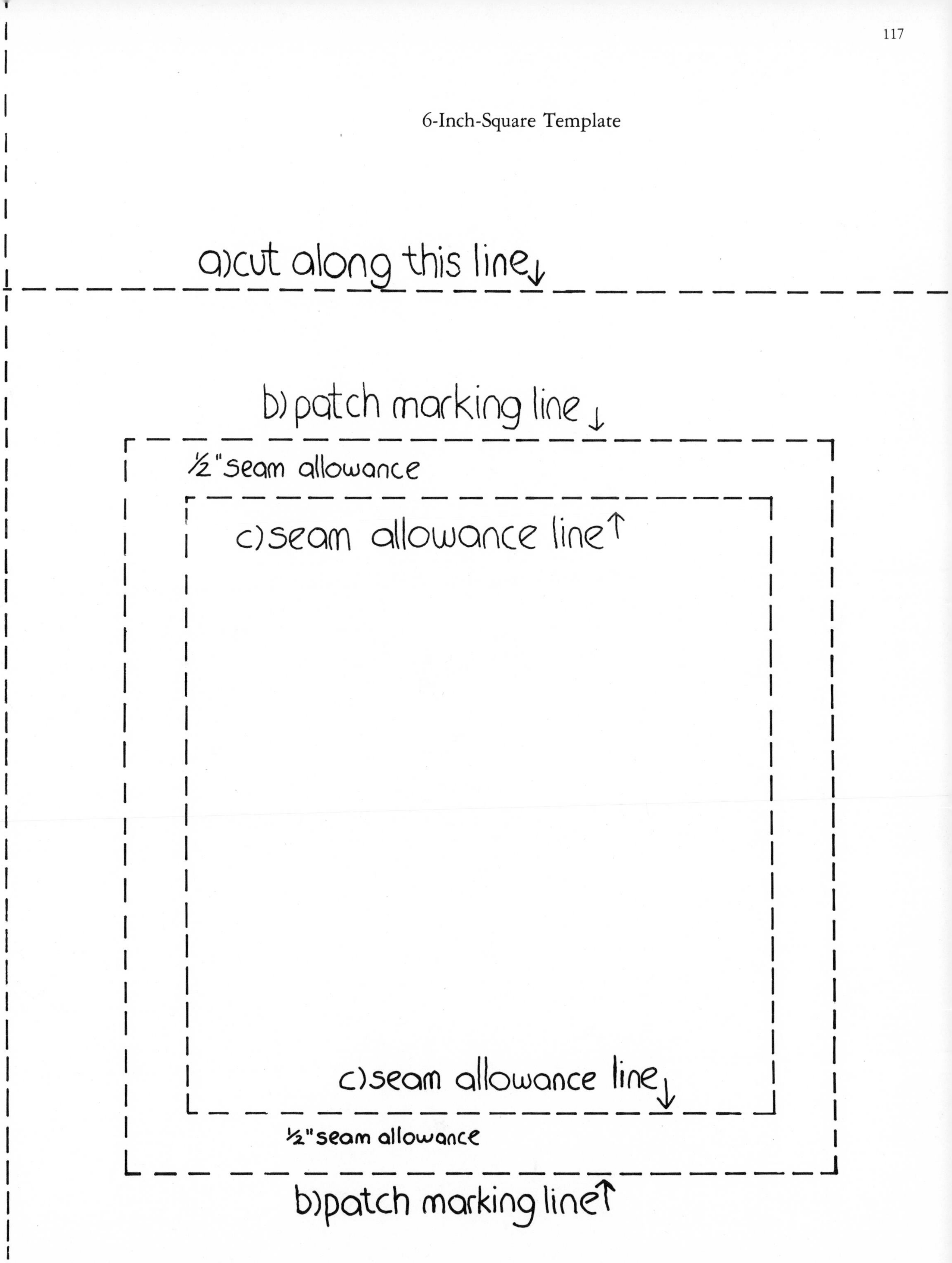

a)cut along this line↓

b) patch marking line ↓

½"seam allowance

c)seam allowance line↑

c)seam allowance line↓

½"seam allowance

b)patch marking line↑

5-Inch-Square Template

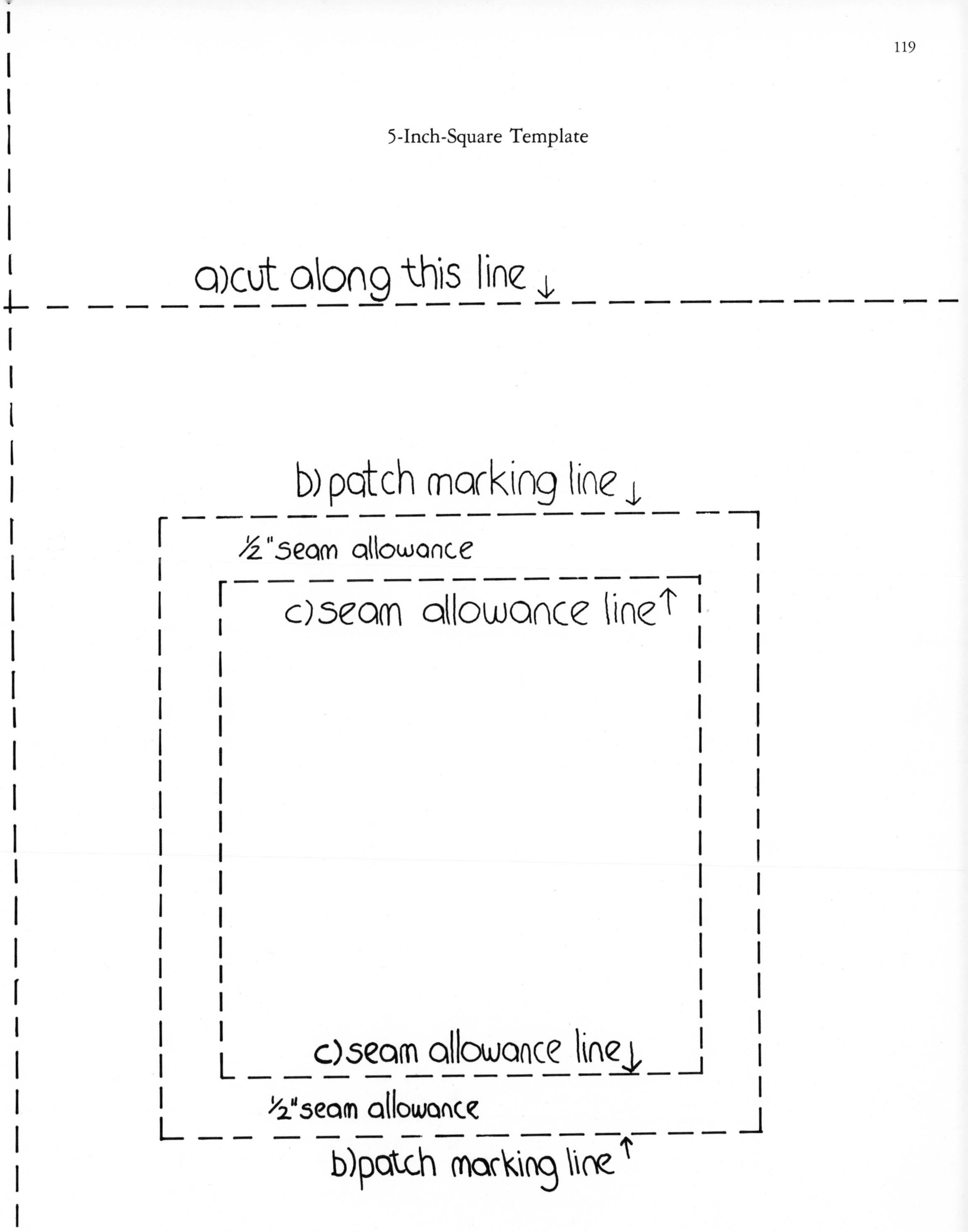

a) cut along this line ↓

b) patch marking line ↓

½" seam allowance

c) seam allowance line ↑

c) seam allowance line ↓

½" seam allowance

b) patch marking line ↑

a) cut along this line →

4-Inch-Square Template

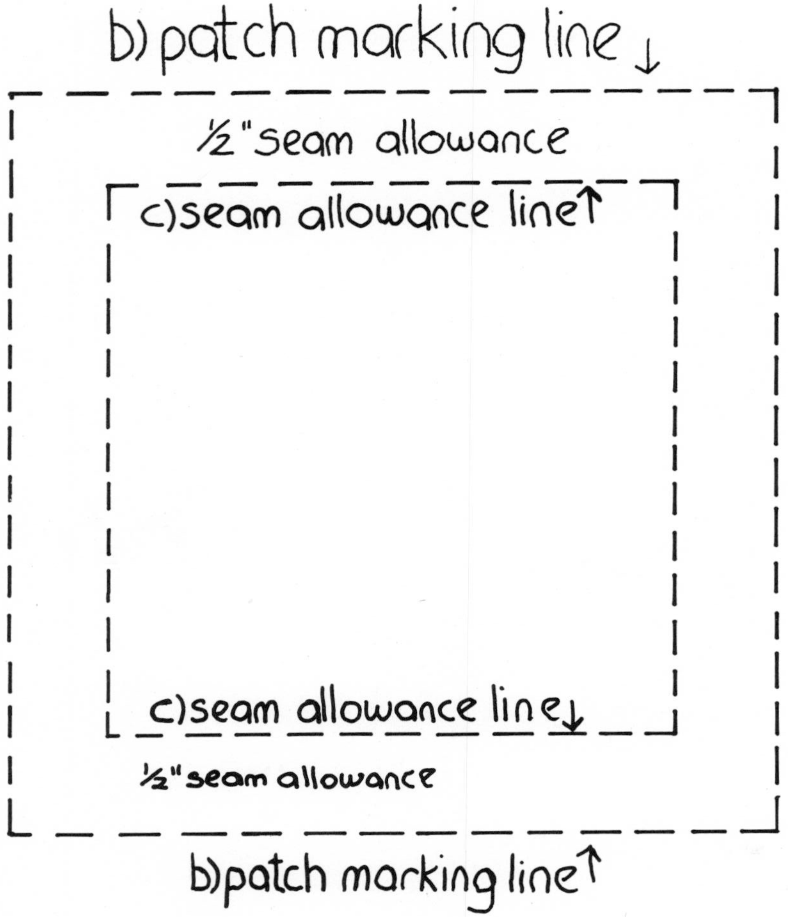

b) patch marking line ↓

½" seam allowance

c) seam allowance line ↑

c) seam allowance line ↓

½" seam allowance

b) patch marking line ↑

3-Inch-Square Template

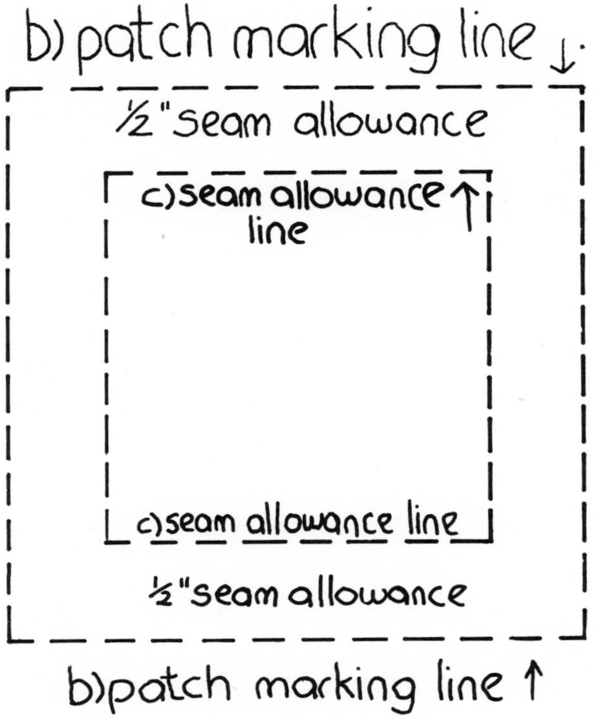

b) patch marking line ↓

½" seam allowance

c) seam allowance line ↑

c) seam allowance line

½" seam allowance

b) patch marking line ↑

Cut-Out Graph Paper

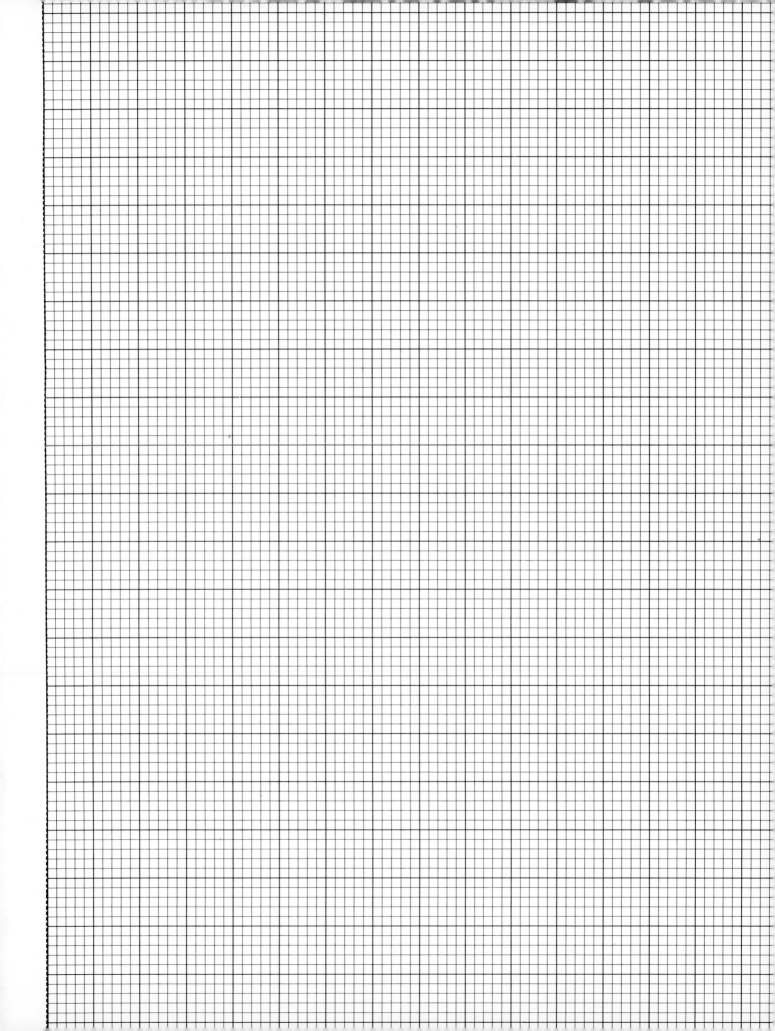

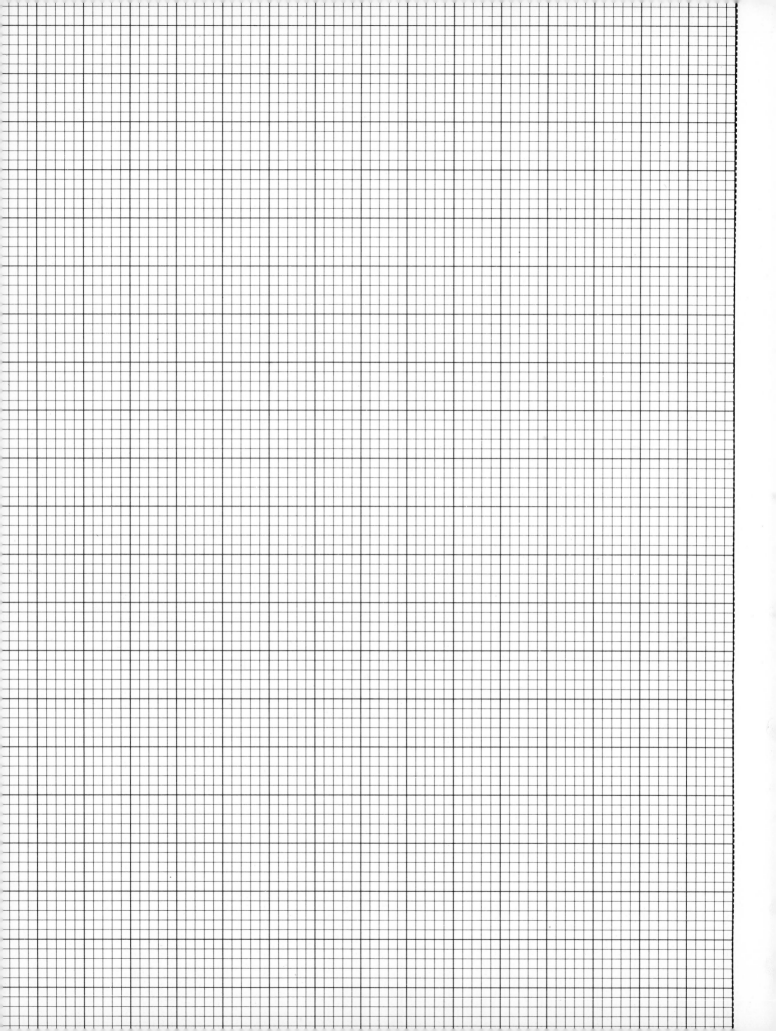

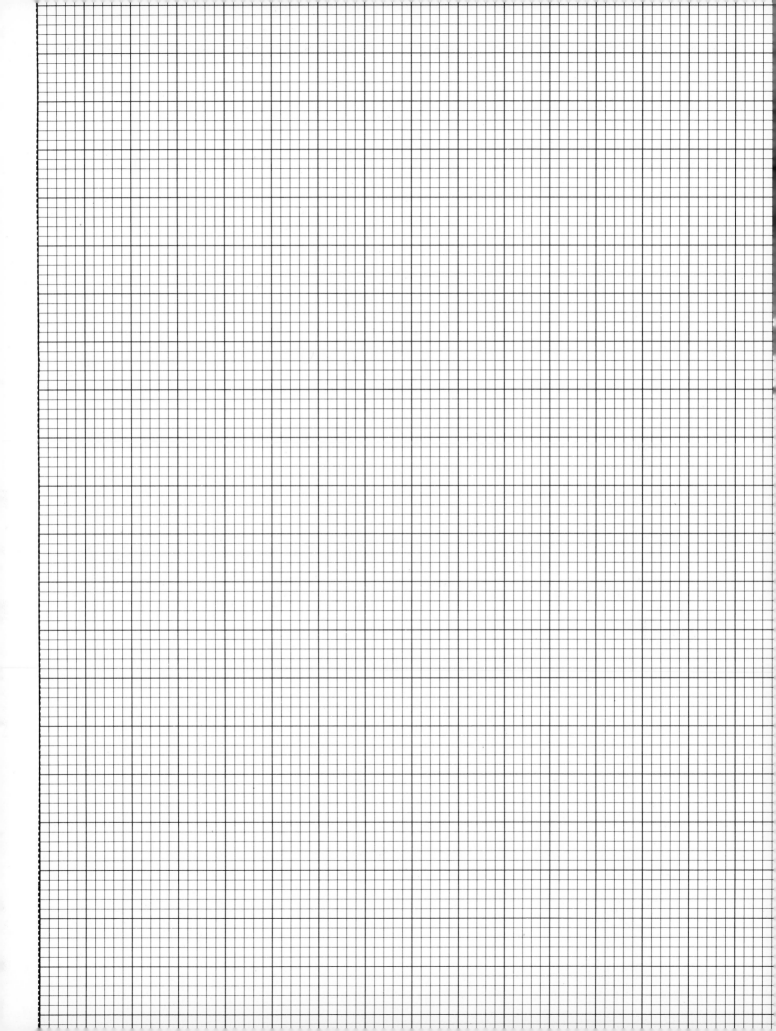

Index